S0-ADQ-477

"Candy is a special person. The way she dedicates so much time and effort to help others is, to me, the greatest form of being Christ here on Earth. My grandpa taught me that it doesn't matter who we are or what we have . . . it's what we do for others that matters. Candy is putting hands and feet to that lesson."

—**Jason Crabb**, Grammy® Award-winning recording artist

on the
other side

on the other side

Life-Changing

Stories from

Under the

Bridge

Candy Christmas

LEAFWOOD
PUBLISHERS

ON THE OTHER SIDE
Life-Changing Stories from Under the Bridge

LEAFWOOD
PUBLISHERS

Copyright 2010 by Candy Christmas

ISBN 978-0-89112-043-8

Printed in the United States of America

ALL RIGHTS RESERVED
No part of this publication may be reproduced, stored in a retrieval system, or transmitted in any form by any means—electronic, mechanical, photocopying, recording or otherwise—without prior written consent. Scripture quotations, unless otherwise noted, are from The Holy Bible, New King James Version. Copyright © 1982 by Thomas Nelson, Inc. Used by permission. All rights reserved.

Scripture quotations noted KJV are taken from the King James Version.

Scripture quotations noted NIV are taken from the New International Version®. Copyright © 1973, 1978, 1984 Biblica®. Used by permission of Zondervan. All rights reserved.

Cover design by Greg Jackson
Interior text design by Sandy Armstrong

Leafwood Publishers
1626 Campus Court
Abilene, Texas 79601
1-877-816-4455 toll free

For current information about all Leafwood titles, visit our Web site:
www.leafwoodpublishers.com

10 11 12 13 14 15 / 7 6 5 4 3 2 1

Dedication

*To my husband, Kent, and to my children
for living these pages with me.*

*To my brother, Trent Hemphill, and Al Jaynes
for convincing me to write these stories down.*

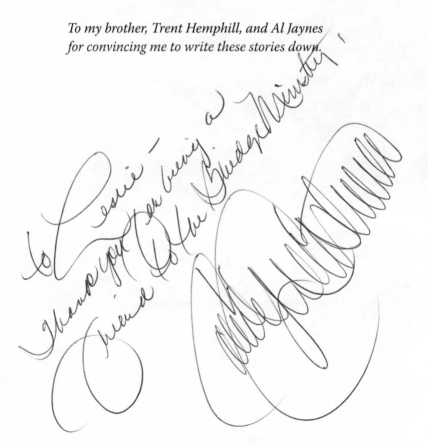

Acknowledgements

The Bridge Ministry Volunteers—for your tireless work and humble hearts in serving the poor.

Church and Ministry Partners—who caught the vision and contributed to bring the vision into reality.

Gary and Kristen Myers—for having a heart for The Bridge, and for helping to prompt the writing of this book.

Denny Boultinghouse—for your wonderful editing job!

Chuck Webster—They say that a picture is worth a thousand words, and each amazing picture you take says more than I could ever write down.

Tara Jackson and Jasmine Christmas Brady—for all your hard work, long hours, and for carrying the burden of the message until it was told.

Table of Contents

The Bridge Builder
by Will Allen Dromgoole

An old man going a lone highway,
Came, at the evening cold and gray,
To a chasm vast and deep and wide.
The old man crossed in the twilight dim,
The sullen stream had no fear for him;
But he turned when safe on the other side
And built a bridge to span the tide.

"Old man," said a fellow pilgrim near,
"You are wasting your strength with building here;
Your journey will end with the ending day,
You never again will pass this way;
You've crossed the chasm, deep and wide,
Why build this bridge at evening tide?"

The builder lifted his old gray head;
"Good friend, in the path I have come," he said,
"There followed after me today
A youth whose feet must pass this way.
This chasm that has been as naught to me
To that fair-haired youth may a pitfall be;
He, too, must cross in the twilight dim;
Good friend, I am building this bridge for him!"

© Public Domain

Speak up for those who cannot speak for themselves,
for the rights of all who are destitute.
Speak up and judge fairly;
defend the rights of the poor and needy.

Proverbs 31: 8, 9 (NIV)

Introduction

As long as I can remember, I have had a desire to help the helpless, to feed the poor, and to champion those whose voice is not heard. For many years I have talked to God alone in my car or while walking on a cold morning. I look to the sky and tell him, "Lord, I don't know where they are." I remember driving the streets of Nashville searching for the place I knew that God had for me, a starting place.

The first time this desire was confirmed in my heart was thirty years ago while traveling with my family singing gospel music. I became consumed with a plan to house the homeless, battered women, and unwed mothers. I couldn't sleep, and I didn't want to take time to eat. All I could do was plan this vision that God had given me. During this time, my family had a concert in downtown Little Rock, Arkansas, at the civic center. Before the evening concert, I found my dad sitting in the front of the bus we were traveling in and asked him if we could talk. I sat down next to him and began to expound on what I felt God was saying to me. I felt driven by this plan and needed to tell someone. I began to unfold every detail—all the dreams of corporate sponsor- ships and how I wanted local congregations to be involved. My dad listened patiently. Helping me with what wisdom he had on the subject, the time flew.

Suddenly I realized that I had talked right up to concert time. I was sitting there in my jeans, no make-up, hair disheveled, and only a few moments away from standing on a stage before a live audience to sing. I ran to my room on the bus, jumped into a dress, quickly brushed my hair and powdered my nose, slipped into my heels, and away I ran. I entered the backstage door with my heart pounding.

Out of the corner of my eye, I could see a very sweet-faced, middle-aged woman who appeared to be waiting for me. She seemed very nervous, probably because I came in the door moving like a locomotive, and she could tell I didn't want to stop for conversation. She stepped into my pathway and asked, "Can I talk to you for a moment?" Out of breath, I stopped as she tried to hand me a hundred dollar bill. I quickly protested, and said, "No ma'am, I am being paid to be here tonight. I can't take your money." Still holding her money out to me, she said, "I am the founder of the Dorcas House here in Little Rock. I care for unwed mothers, battered women, foster children, and the homeless. The Lord spoke to me in prayer that I should come tell you that he wants to use you in this type of ministry in the years to come, and I am to sow this money into your ministry for the future."

I was completely floored! The Lord sent this dear lady to confirm all that he had put in my heart, and all that my dad and I had discussed. I understood how much the Dorcas House needed the money that she had given me, and I tried very hard to give it back to her. I feared God too much to take her money and spend it on frivolous things that an eighteen-year-old girl like me might buy such as nail polish, pantyhose, or a new outfit. After her constant refusals, I took her money and gave it back to the Lord through another ministry in Nashville. I planted it in the field of the Lord with faith that God would bless the Dorcas House for their sacrifice, and that he would bring to reality the vision he had placed in my heart.

It would be many years before I would find the place God had for me on the streets, and I am still on a journey to do more: to help more people and to house the poor. I never forgot that night in Little Rock, or the word "in season" spoken to me by that precious woman from the Dorcus House. Like Mary, I still ponder these things in my heart (Luke 2:19).

Chapter One

On the Other Side

Prelude

I like to think of myself as an adventurous soul. Don't get me wrong, I like traveling within my sphere of comfort, like the next guy. But there have been landmark times in my life when I knew that God was leading me to embark on new journeys, to destinations unknown. Times when it took great faith to leave my place of safety and travel uncharted waters. "Man cannot discover new oceans unless he has the courage to lose sight of the shore" (André Gide).

One year at Christmas, Kent, my husband, and I bought a little red wagon for our son, Nicholas. It was a Radio Flyer with a bold white lightning bolt painted down the side. Nicholas was absolutely thrilled as he ripped the wrapping paper from around it and realized what it was. He could hardly wait for spring to arrive to take it for a spin. As soon as the weather was nice, he and our daughter Jasmine began to beg me to pull them through the neighborhood in it. They loved to pile into the wagon with our dogs in their laps, and away we'd go, up and down our street.

It didn't take long to realize why "little red wagons" have lost some of their popularity. It occurred to me that while someone is enjoying a wonderful ride, there has to be someone else out front pulling. That would be me. We live in Tennessee and our neighborhood terrain is very hilly. There is no level stretch of road, only up and down. What started out as good ole family fun wound up as a vigorous work out for me, and I worked up a good old-fashioned sweat. It was about that time that a brilliant idea hit my brain. I am certain I never processed it through my thought filter, but I began to try to convince my kids that we could all ride together in the little red wagon. Wouldn't it be fun for me to climb in the wagon with them and ride down our driveway together!

Our home is built on the side of a steep hill with the driveway built on a sharp downward slope. Halfway down the driveway is a sharp 180 degree turn back. I surmised that the long tongue of the wagon could be pulled back so that a passenger could steer, and I, being the experienced driver of course, would be in charge of navigating.

Standing at the top of the driveway, however, and looking down the vertical slope in front of them, my little cohorts became leery of our plan. After much pleading, I finally convinced them that I knew exactly what I was doing, and there was nothing to fear in our little adventure. Reluctantly they climbed in.

We started down the driveway, picking up speed with every second. I'm sure to any onlooker (I hope there weren't any) that little red wagon looked like the red tail of a meteor being flung to the earth. Squeals of excitement instantly turned to screams of terror, as I realized the little red Radio Flyer was spinning out of control. My weight, along with the high rate of speed at which we were moving, caused the tongue to be stuck in place so that I couldn't steer. With a sharp right turn in our path, I had no choice but to jerk the tongue with all my strength to the left. I used such force that we all toppled over and went rolling down the pavement.

There we all were lying in the middle of the driveway with our knees and elbows skinned and bruised. My favorite jeans were torn at the knees, and there was no part of my body that didn't hurt; and in the distance I could hear Nicholas yelling that he thought his leg was broken (thankfully it wasn't). For a moment I was dazed and lay there looking up at the sky thinking, "Wow! How did that happen?" I slowly stood to my feet to assess the damage, feeling like a moron for putting my children in harm's way.

Several years later while at the peak of my career, again I found myself on a ride of more epic proportions that too was spiraling out of control. My dreams of success were being fulfilled and I was singing to audiences of thousands a night and flying on a private jet. While at the pinnacle of my achievements, I found myself in the darkest place

I had ever known. I was tormented by a cloud so evil and demonic that words can hardly describe it. I lost my appetite and lost a dramatic amount of weight, losing down to one hundred pounds. I have read medical studies that say that depression is anger turned inward. Although I had reached some measure of accomplishment, I was angry at myself and God that I had not reached higher and achieved more. At this point I believe that no measure of success could have satisfied my craving. I felt that I had fallen into an abyss, that Satan had taken my mind and my very soul. I remember on several occasions walking through coliseums and asking myself, "I'm dead aren't I?"

With my emotions raw, I knew that I was on the verge of a mental breakdown and needed help. The joyride had become a nightmare, and now my little red wagon of dreams was lying on its side with the wheels still spinning. I went to see Dr. James Miller, my doctor and friend for many years. I remember him telling me, "Candy, you are severely depressed." He wrote prescriptions for me of sedatives and antidepressants, and wanted to hospitalize me. He told me that I must cancel my upcoming concerts, and wrote a doctor's order that was to be sent to the promoters to cancel events. To be honest, I barely remember this time; I was dazed and asking myself, "How did this happen?" A deep darkness had settled over my mind and I was trying to hold to any shred of sanity. I remember my husband, Kent, and my brothers, Trent and Joey, taking charge and emptying my calendar and canceling concerts. All I wanted to do was lie in bed in the dark with the curtains drawn and ache from the depths of my soul. And I did. I prayed to die; I embraced the thought of suicide and planned my funeral. I had two small children still living at home, and thank God, I had the presence of mind to know that they would never be the same from such a blow, so I settled on the fact that death was not an option. There I lay, day after day, week after week. I couldn't die, and I couldn't live. I was suspended somewhere between life and death, going through the motions, walking the earth like a zombie.

My husband is a man of prayer. He has a tremendous strength in God that I admire greatly. I remember that he entered my room every afternoon about the same time. He opened the blinds, and gently placed his hands on me and began to pray. When I couldn't pray for myself, he prayed for me. It was as if I could feel the virtue and spirit of Christ flowing into me as he prayed.

After some time the dark cloud began to lift. Even though I was still shaking and unsure of myself, I began to enter life again. But still, my constant companion was an inward anger. I could see it in my countenance in family photos, and in moments of solitude and reflection I seethed with resentment. Often friends asked me, "Are you angry with me?" Much to my amazement, I hadn't realized that it was obvious. Every day during my personal devotional time, I began to pray against this anger in my life. I was raised in a denomination where we believed everything was the devil. I began to pray and quote the scripture, "What things I bind on earth shall be bound in heaven." I prayed, "You devil of anger that is tormenting me, I bind you." All the while, I became angrier.

One day I was praying, working hard at binding the devil, when all of a sudden I stopped. I looked up to heaven and said, "Lord, this is not working!" I got very quiet before the Lord and heard the still voice inside me say, "You are angry because you are fighting against my will. When you rest in my will for your life, you will no longer be angry." I realized that I was angry with God because he hadn't allowed me to be the "star" I thought I should be. I believed that I was groomed and destined for greatness, and the world was waiting for my appearance on center stage. Here I find myself, with no career, no ministry, just being a mom, and I was angry.

It was there, in my prayer closet, that I told the Lord, "Not my will but thy will be done." I told the Lord, "If your will for my life is that I live in a tent in China, and pass out tracts on a street corner, I will do it. Jesus Christ is enough for me." It was there in that moment that my desire for a stage and spotlight was crucified, and I became willing to trade it all and take up my cross. It was there that my craving for applause and accolades died, and a grace to embrace the will of God for my life was born. I had prayed so many times, "Lord, let me die. I don't want to live." He heard me and answered my prayer. "For I am crucified with Christ, nevertheless I live . . . yet not I, but Christ in me." I left behind the safety of the plans that I had made and allowed the wind of the Holy Spirit to fill my sails. Little did I know that God was taking me on the journey of a lifetime. I had no idea of the beautiful people I would come to know under a bridge who were waiting for me . . . *On the Other Side.*

From a Pot of Jambalaya

I am a southern girl from Louisiana, born into a pastor's home where southern hospitality was an everyday part of life. Most of our social activities, church functions, and family gatherings were centered around huge pots of gumbo or long tables of pot luck. It was the norm that in the planning of any event the first question asked would be, "What will we eat?" or "What do you want me to bring?"

I am still very much a southern girl, and thrive on cooking for any size crowd. I never feel completely satisfied until I have fed anyone who comes to my door, be it a stray cat or dog, friend or television repairman. My daughter-in-law Carrie affectionately calls me a "food pusher" because from the moment she walks in the door until the time she leaves, I am trying to feed her. My husband says that he can measure how long we have known each of our friends by how much weight they have gained. Which is just fine by me.

After the pain of my depression had lifted and my schedule slowed, I went through a season in which a new Candy Christmas emerged. I enjoyed rediscovering myself and past interests I had not had time to pursue. I enjoyed homemaking and most of all I loved being with my husband and children again. I found new joy in preparing meals, baking bread, decorating cakes, and making Christmas candies through the holidays. My home became full of laughter and joy once more. I began to plan events and invite guests to our home for dinner, then every waking moment leading to their arrival was spent preparing. One day I was explaining this process of entertaining to my Aunt Rita, and out of the blue she remarked, "I have never heard of anyone preparing for one meal for three days—it is eaten in only thirty minutes. Somehow this must be the Lord. I believe that God wants to use this in your life." I was taken aback by this statement, and later thought of it often. How could God use my desire to feed people? I called a culinary school here in Nashville to begin the process of enrolling.

Soon the Lord began to show me throughout his Word how he uses the natural talents and abilities of a person to guide them in their work for him. Paul was a tent maker by trade (Acts 18:3). He was skilled and for many years painstakingly worked to prepare dwellings. God used this man, with his knowledge of building, to build the kingdom of God through his teachings.

Peter was a fisherman by trade. He spent the early part of his life casting nets and catching large droughts of fish. Jesus used this analogy when he called Peter to be his disciple, saying, ". . . I will make you fishers of men" (Matt. 4:19). In Acts 2 on the day of Pentecost, Peter stood and preached his first message and three thousand souls were saved that day. The fisherman became the soul winner.

When the time had come for Moses to fulfill the purpose for which he was born, God asked, "Moses, what is that in your hand?" (Exod. 4:2, NIV). All he had was a staff. He was no longer in the home of Pharaoh, where at one time he could have replied, "Lord, I have gold, I have power." All he had to offer God was a dirty, old stick.

Our homeless friends lining up for the meal

I knew that God wasn't finished with my life, but I still believed that I could only be effective through my singing talents. When I became hugely successful some day in the by and by, then I could help the poor. With my ministry and my career at a standstill, it never occurred to me that God wanted to use what was in my hand . . . today.

During this time, some of my relatives were building a new home. They had hired a minister to lay their tile, and I had met him on a couple of occasions. In the course of the conversation, he told me that he had been going under a bridge downtown, where many homeless people lived, to grill hamburgers and share the gospel with them. He asked me if I'd like to go. I was completely fascinated by this idea and immediately said, "Yes!" He looked at me sheepishly out of the corner of his eye and asked, "Can you cook?" I could tell by his tone of voice that he was sure I could not. I said, "Yes, I'm a Louisiana girl, and I can cook jambalaya in any size pot, for any size crowd." He grinned in disbelief and said, "Okay, how about next Tuesday?" I agreed.

When Tuesday rolled around, I was ready. I had prepared a large pot of chicken and sausage jambalaya and drove to the bridge. I had no idea what I would encounter, so my heart pounded. I wasn't sure if my life would be in danger, if I might be robbed, or worse, so at first I kept my distance.

Looking back to that first night under the bridge, I realize that the homeless people that I met were as apprehensive of me as I was of them. There were only a few who came to be served that night, but as they formed a line to receive the food I had brought, my heart was broken. This was January, and a very cold, dark evening. Shame kept many of them from looking into my eyes, but much gratitude was shown by the many thanks I received. They were dirty and cold, some had no coat or gloves, and as I watched them walk away, I could see that most had no socks in their shoes to warm their feet. Suddenly, it became clear to me what was in my hand. It wasn't a microphone, or an autograph pen, or my last CD, but it was the love of Jesus. Real, true love that cannot be explained. A love that has burned deeply within my heart since that first night under the bridge. The kind of love that has given me the grace to weather the cold. A love that is able to embrace those who have the smell of urine in their clothes or the smell of alcohol on their breath. Love that looks at the last few years on the streets as if it were only a moment, and leads me forward with joy to the years ahead.

I believe that God is waiting for us to see what is in our hands today, whether it is a needle for tentmaking, a fishing pole, a dirty stick, or a pot of jambalaya. When we recognize it, and throw it down, there is a blessing...*On the Other Side.*

Chapter Two

Orphans of God

Prelude

There are no strangers,
There are no outcasts,
There are no orphans of God.
So many fallen, but hallelujah,
there are no orphans of God . . . .

© Joel Lindsey/Twila LaBar / Bridge Building Music /
Upright Grand Music / BMI

At Christmastime, when my husband was twelve years old, he was awakened in the middle of the night to the sound of his mother crying. Getting up from his bed, he sleepily stumbled into the family room to find it filled with family members and close friends. He began making his way through the crowded room to the place his mother was seated when he was intercepted by a minister. He was then informed that his father had passed away unexpectedly, and it was then that Kent's life changed forever.

Charlie Christmas, Kent's dad, was a missionary to the Quinault Indians. He had moved his family onto the reservation, where he pastored a small church and often hunted game with the Indians. There wasn't much money in that line of work, so he left few assets behind. The most treasured of his possessions that Kent inherited was his father's Bible, the one from which he preached. Kent struggled with loneliness and feelings of abandonment for many years after his dad passed away. His mother had fallen into depression from being widowed by the love of her life, and could offer him little emotional support. He often retreated to his dad's Bible for comfort, and at times it became his closest friend.

At the age of seventeen, Kent answered the call to ministry and began preaching from this priceless heirloom. When I met him some years later, that Bible was well worn and still in full use. After we married Kent accepted a preaching engagement in Memphis, Tennessee, that would include an overnight stay. We had checked into a local motel and after that night's church service we locked our car and went inside for the night. Early the next morning, with our suitcases in our hands, we strolled to the parking lot to load the car. Much to our disbelief, we found that the car had been stolen with Kent's dad's Bible inside. He was devastated! At that moment, the car was secondary and the loss of the Bible became our main focus. Even though the leather cover of the Bible was faded, the pages were tattered, and the binding was loose, it meant the world to Kent. To him the old ragged Bible was of greater value than the car or anything else left in it. We began to pray earnestly. I'm not sure if we ever asked the Lord for the recovery of the car, but we bombarded heaven for the Bible!

Amazingly enough, the car was found a couple of days later, abandoned in an obscure parking lot on the other side of Memphis. It had been stripped and ransacked, and all of our belongings that had been left inside it were gone—except the Bible. It had been badly damaged, the leather was scorched and shriveled, but that didn't matter to us. The thieves had taken all that they had found to be valuable, but had left the one thing that was the most precious and dear to us.

After its recovery, Kent never preached from his dad's Bible again. We carefully placed it in a box for safekeeping and displayed it in a prominent place in our home. With its shriveled cover and frayed pages, we are proud to show it to our guests who come to visit.

My grandmother had a saying, "Never judge a book by its cover," and now I guess I know why. It seems to be a natural human tendency to judge the value of things by the outward appearance, even people. We observe whether or not they are handsome, well groomed, or wearing stylish clothes, then we often form our opinions on first impression or outward appearance. The Bible warns us against the practice of favoring one who has fine clothing. We should not say to him, "You sit here in a good place," and say to the poor man, "You stand there," or, "Sit here at my footstool" (James 2:1-4).

We see the Old Testament affirm that "For the LORD does not see as man sees; for man looks at the outward appearance, but the LORD looks at the heart" (1 Sam. 16:7). God sent the prophet Samuel to the house of Jesse to anoint one of Jesse's sons as king. Samuel's eyes fell on Eliab, and he instantly assumed that he was God's choice because of his stature and good looks, when in fact God had rejected him.

Outward appearance can often be deceiving. On the one hand, we meet those who are considered the upper echelon of society and lauded as "great," but whom we later find are very "small." On the other hand, we see those who some consider the "dregs of society" who possess excellent character. I am glad that our heavenly Father has no caste system. He loves and welcomes "whosoever will" and will accept us no matter our race, financial portfolio, education, or station in life.

Most of us have suffered rejection on some level, at one point or other in our lives. Quite possibly we too were misjudged by our "cover" or by some outward impediment beyond our control. Maybe a bad case of acne as a teen prevented you from getting a date to the prom. As for me, I was the fat kid in sixth grade, who weighed in at a whopping one hundred and fifty pounds. Believe me when I say that I heard every fat joke imaginable, and I suffered cruelly. Others encounter more serious life-altering calamities that leave them with feelings of rejection, such as being fired from a job, a divorce, or the death of a loved one. Then some of us suffer from self-inflicted wounds. Bad choices and mistakes in judgment can cost us valuable relationships and leave us feeling demoralized and alone.

Whatever the circumstance, our souls have now been forever branded with the mark of suffering, and we are left with two choices. Do I become the victim, or do I become victorious? I, for one, have chosen to get up from my coffin of self pity and shake off the grave clothes the enemy tried to bury me in. I have decided that my empathy would be better served by using it for someone who really needed it—someone other than myself. I refuse to afford myself the luxury of sitting around licking my wounds. I have found out first hand that is counterproductive, and anyway, it left an awful taste in my mouth. There's a whole world out there full of hurting people who need to be touched by some loving soul who can identify with their pain.

Have you noticed that we human beings have become very adept at disguising our true identities? We often would rather mask our personal defects by hiding behind success or material possessions, instead of allowing the Holy Spirit to change us into the image of Christ. We build stone walls around our hearts to guard our weaknesses, yet the walls we've built for protection also deflect love that we so desperately desire. Sadly, we often attend church smiling broadly, while walking through troubling situations. We needlessly isolate ourselves from those who care, hoping that our struggles won't be exposed. All the while we are inwardly longing for the embrace of a friend, someone to say, "I'm praying for you."

Scientists say that the human body is designed to heal itself. If you gash your finger, your body will instantly begin forming a scab to protect the wound. It's the same way with Christ's body. When our brothers and sisters in Christ are injured and suffering, God has put it in us to run to their aide and cover the injury with love and prayer, "bear one another's burdens" (Gal. 6:2). I don't know where I would be today without Christian relationships and prayer partners who prayed for me when I didn't have the strength to pray for myself—those who ran to my rescue and covered my injuries, even when some were self-inflicted.

In the Gospel of Luke (22:31–32), Jesus addressed Simon Peter: "Simon! Indeed, Satan has asked for you, that he may sift you as wheat. But I have prayed for you, that your faith should not fail; and when you have returned to Me, strengthen your brethren." If you ever do much baking, chances are that sooner or later you will use a sifter. A sifter is used for aerating flour, so that your biscuits will be fluffy or your cakes lighter. Another thing a sifter does is separate the debris or clumps from fine flour. Pour the flour into the sifter and begin to turn the handle. The fine flour is sifted and falls through the screen mesh, and only the debris or "bad" remains. What Christ was telling Peter was that Satan wanted to put his life in a sifter and sift him until all the good fell away and only the bad remained.

God doesn't sift, he shakes (Heb. 12:27). He shakes those things that can be shaken so that "the things which cannot be shaken may remain." Sometimes God allows us to be shaken so that, in the process, we find ourselves reevaluating our walk with him. Before you realize it, the "bad" has fallen away and only the "good" remains. When I go through trials in my life, I stop to ask myself, "Is this God shaking, or the enemy of my soul trying to sift?" When this question is answered, then I pray accordingly.

Jesus told Peter that Satan desired to sift him, but that Jesus had prayed for his faith. The original definition of the word *sift* is this: "Inward agitation to try one's faith to the verge of overthrow" (*Strong's*

"There are no strangers...."

4617). Satan saw Peter's value to God, and he desired to overthrow his faith to render him useless. Many of the homeless have gone through a sifting, and Satan has successfully overthrown their faith. Their families are fragmented, their bodies are broken, and their dreams and goals exchanged for bottles and syringes. Many are depressed and disillusioned, angry with God and society for all that life has dealt them. You might be thinking: I understand why Satan would want to overthrow Peter's faith. He was one of Jesus' disciples, he preached powerfully on the day of Pentecost. He healed the sick, and wrote two books in the New Testament. But homeless people? Why does the devil care about some old drunk or drug addict who lives under a bridge? Why would he waste his time overthrowing their faith?

Remember, we have been talking about judging a book by its cover. We decided that you can't always judge value by the outward appearance. Could it be that the greatest damage to the kingdom of darkness might come from someone whose faith was overthrown by it? Maybe we aren't only talking about the homeless here; this also applies to the wealthy and affluent, the guy who trades on Wall Street who is hooked on crack cocaine; or the attorney who hides a bottle in his desk drawer at the office to help him through the day. People who have isolated themselves and feel orphaned and abandoned by their transgressions. These can be the most valuable tools in the hand of God. Could it be that people who have been to hell and back are great with directions? Could they be the ones who know their way to the gates of hell to storm them and lead others out?

In the Gospel of John (14:18), Jesus once said, "I will not leave you comfortless . . . ." Interestingly, the word "comfortless" is the Greek word "orphaned"(*Strong's* 3737). "I will not leave you orphans." There are no outcasts, there are no . . . *Orphans of God.*

Bobby's Coat

The ministry to the homeless had grown to such a point that we had given it a name: The Bridge Ministry. After only a few months into our work with the poor, we leased our first little warehouse, excited to see all the ways that God would fill it. We had received our first truckload of coats and winter was approaching, but we had very little provision for food.

There is a small town nearby that is home to a small food bank, where a friend of ours is CEO, Pastor Ron Stroupe. Kent and I love this man dearly and greatly admire his work with the needy. An unwritten code of brotherhood among most Christian non-profit organizations is that we do all we can to help each other. When I have an abundance of certain items, I call ministries who may need our surplus, and vice versa. At this particular time I was the "new kid." I had much need and nothing to share in return, so there I stood asking for a hand-out from these other ministries.

Pastor Ron had mercy on my zeal, and took me under his wing a bit to teach me the ropes. One day he called to tell me that he was making a trip to the regional food bank, and asked Kent and me if we would like to go. This was a dream come true for me, so when we arrived I could only walk around in amazement with my jaw dropped. It was like Disneyland to me or Sam's Club gone hyper-space. Pastor Ron took us into the office and introduced us to all the "powers that be." He helped us with our application and was our reference so that we could begin to place orders.

Pastor Ron had also invited us to take our box truck that day. He said that he wanted to apply our first truckload of food to his account, and not only did he pay for our food, but he brought a young man to help us load. When we were finished with our shopping, the plan was that we'd all go back to the warehouse to unpack. I was elated and overwhelmed at the kindness of Pastor Ron; he was, and still is, an extraordinary friend.

As the day rocked on, the adrenaline from "grocery-shopping on steroids" faded, and then came the task of unloading all we had bought. As we began the task, I became better acquainted with Bobby, the young man whom Ron had brought to help me. He was a nice looking young man with a natural curl in his hair, which gave him a boyish appearance. He looked to be in his mid twenties, but if you looked more closely at the lines on his face, you could see that he had met with hard times in his young life. He was very polite and a hard worker, and Kent and I instantly liked him.

We had heard from Pastor Ron that Bobby had battled drug addiction for a long time, but had not been able to overcome temptation, due in part to geography. He would be clean for a while, but because he was not able to leave his environment, he would fall back into his old habits. Someone had offered to let him stay in a small camper trailer in this little town of White House where Pastor Ron lived, and there he stayed, trying to begin a new life. My heart broke for him, and by the end of the day, we had forged a friendship.

The weather was quite cold already, and as we worked together that day, I realized that Bobby wasn't wearing a coat, and actually had on short sleeves. I heard him sniffle when it dawned on me and I instantly asked, "Bobby! Where is your coat?" "I don't have a coat," he answered. I gently took his arm and led him to a corner of the warehouse where I had boxes of new coats stacked to the ceiling. I eagerly searched through the sizes until I came to what looked to be his size. I tore it out of the plastic and helped him try it on. It was a perfect fit. He looked so handsome, and he was very proud to be wearing a brand new jacket.

At the end of the day, our little warehouse was bulging, we were exhausted, and it was time to say good-bye to Pastor Ron and our newfound friend Bobby. We thanked them both, and hugged them with promises of seeing each other again. The end of a perfect day.

Pastor Ron later told me that when they got into his little truck to make the journey back to White House, Bobby was noticeably quiet. After some time had passed, Pastor Ron asked, "Bobby, what's on your mind, son. Are you okay?" Bobby replied, "I don't understand it. Why was Candy so nice to me? Why would she give me a coat, when she doesn't know me?" Then he was quiet again.

Pastor Ron saw this as a wonderful opportunity to tell him about the love of Jesus. "Jesus loves you so much, and he uses people to show you his love." Pastor Ron talked with him about Jesus all the way home. When they parked in the driveway where Bobby's camper trailer was parked, Pastor Ron asked Bobby if he could pray for him, and he gave his consent. They prayed the sinner's prayer together, there in the cab of that little truck, and Bobby gave his heart to the Lord.

Early the next morning I was getting ready for a long day in the office, when my cell phone rang. I read my caller ID and realized that it was Pastor Ron, so I excitedly answered, and began thanking him profusely again and again for all that he had done for us. I soon began to realize that he wasn't responding as he normally would; he had a seriousness in his voice. "Sister, I need to talk with you about Bobby." Again I broke in to tell him how much we enjoyed meeting Bobby. "He hung himself last night, sister," he interrupted. I was stunned. I quietly found a chair and sat down. "What happened?" I gasped. "I'm not sure," he answered. We sat there on the phone in silence for a moment trying to process the news.

Before her death, Mother Teresa was asked about the extreme poverty and starvation she had encountered throughout her ministry, and how God could allow the innocent to suffer. With her feeble voice, week with age, she answered, "When I see Jesus, there are many questions I must ask him."

There are many questions I have about my meeting with Bobby on his last day on planet earth. My mind was tormented with questions for a very long time: "Could I have done more? How could I have better helped him? Why didn't I see the signs? Did God entrust Bobby

"There are no outcasts..."

to our care at this critical time, and I let him down? Did Bobby go to heaven?" These are questions that I can't answer, so I had to commit them to God. I, too, have decided that, "When I see Jesus, there are many questions I must ask him."

Ally's Story

At the close of each of our outreach services, I always try to bring the service to a point where those who have needs or want salvation can receive prayer. Many of our volunteers are veteran Christians whom I've named our "prayer partners." They are skilled in witnessing, and ready to pray with those who come forward with needs.

On a warm summer night, we were nearing the close of our Shelby Street service where we had enjoyed a wonderful church service beneath the stars. I gave the invitation, and I could feel the Holy Spirit tugging at the hearts of the lost as the music played softly, so I paused for a moment to watch God work. Out of the darkness came an emaciated skeletal frame; with tears pouring down her face, she came toward me sobbing and fell on my neck. I held her frail frame for a few moments. "How can I pray for you?" I tenderly asked.

As she answered, I could smell the stench of hard liquor on her breath and instantly detected that she was quite drunk. "I need you to pray and ask God if he will take this alcohol away from me. Ask him to make me stop drinking! The doctor says I'm dying, and I can't stop." Still with my arms around her I asked, "What is your name?" "Ally" was her reply.

"Ally," I began, feeling the leading of the Holy Spirit as I spoke, "I will be happy to pray for you, but I wonder if you would pray with me." I could tell she wanted salvation, and it's my goal to lead those who come to me to a personal dialogue of their own with the Lord. "If you would talk to Jesus and tell him what you need, I know that he will hear you and answer. I will pray along with you."

"Oh, no! I can't do that! I am angry at God, and I'm not speaking to him! You pray for me!" I was obviously surprised by her answer, and instinctively asked, "Angry at God? Why?"

"He let my mother die when I was sixteen, and I had nowhere else to go but to the streets, where I've been homeless ever since. I started drinking when I was sixteen to cope with all the terrible things that have happened to me out here. I am so angry with God!" She broke into deep sobs again, and all I could do was pray. I prayed from the depths of my soul for Ally, as I felt love from the heart of the Father rise inside of me. After some time I was able to lead her in a prayer for salvation.

Ally attends our church services under the bridge regularly, and she is usually very inebriated. Never again have I seen her respond to God, or conduct herself in ways that fundamental Christians would deem acceptable. She stays on the outside perimeter of the crowd, yet I watch as she listens closely to the Word of God. I can still feel the love of the Father for her, and I pray that she will come to know him in a more personal way. I cannot judge, and won't begin to try. I do know that Ally had a true experience with Jesus Christ. I also know that great

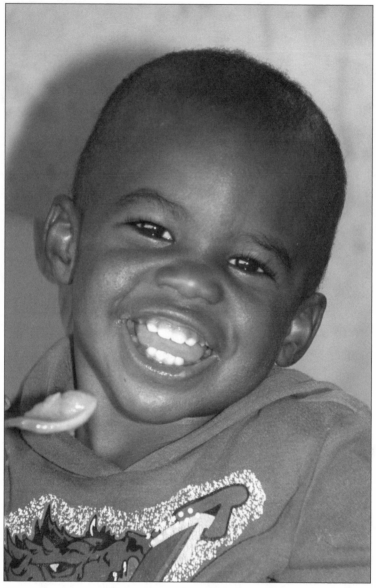

"There are no orphans of God..."

is the mercy of our Lord, who has compassion on this precious one and all the pain that she has endured.

In Ephesians (3:17-18, NIV) the scripture says, "I pray that you . . . may have power, together with all the saints, to grasp how wide and long and high and deep is the love of Christ," for wondering souls like Ally, who feel that they are . . . *Orphans of God.*

Nashville Connection

"If such a thing as grace exists,
then grace was made for lives like this . . ."

Since I have been under the bridge, I have come across many people who are not homeless because they want to be, but because life has brought them difficult circumstances. These people have been through great tragedies and trials which they can't seem to overcome— and won't overcome unless God intervenes. I think that often we look at men and women standing on the side of the road holding their signs and immediately put them in our "homeless category," never thinking that these people have a family and a story. I want to share a few of their stories with you, so that maybe you can better understand.

Jake's Story

From time to time there are Christian artists who tell the stories of The Bridge Ministry in their concerts to raise awareness for our cause. One particular gospel artist who has become a vital part of the ministry had at one point taken a homeless man into his home to help him get back on his feet. He and his family cared for the man as their own family member, and offered him a job playing guitar in their band.

One evening, while in concert in Dalton, Georgia, they introduced their guitar player to the congregation as a homeless man, Jake. He performed and was well received by the audience, with a great outpouring of love. The next week, they received a call in their Nashville office from a woman who was a member of the congregation where the concert was held in Georgia. The woman on the line said, "I was unable to attend the concert the evening the group was here, but I watched it online. I really enjoyed your ministry." The woman stated: "The reason I am calling is to inquire about the homeless man, Jake, who was playing the guitar." She said, "You see, my parents had ten children and then divorced when I was very young. I was separated from my brothers and sisters at that time because we were dispersed among foster homes and orphanages. Consequently, I lost all contact with my siblings." She continued, "I have not seen my brothers and sisters since our separation. When I watched the service online, you introduced a homeless man. Much to my amazement you introduced Jake, and I recognized him as my baby brother! I have not seen him since childhood."

With the help of goodhearted people, who believe in second chances, Jake was given a wonderful job opportunity to play in a band. From one act of kindness came restoration to a soul and reunion for a family. Jake was reunited with his sister, and together they found their birthmother; for the first time since Jake's infancy they became a family. There are no outcasts, there are no . . . *Orphan's of God.*

Shadows of the Past

Bruce is a man who has been coming to our services under the bridge since we first began. Quite honestly, he remains the most inebriated human being that I have ever seen who could still stand under his own power. He is a favorite among our volunteers, partly because of his kindness, and partly because we know that he is a veteran who has served our country in the armed forces. Most of us pay special attention to his needs, often carefully seating him and serving him, making sure that he is particularly cared for. During a recent doctor visit, his physician asked him, "Bruce, do you have a burial plot?" "No, I don't," he replied. "You need to buy one. You are killing yourself with the amount of alcohol you are consuming. You won't live much longer."

For years I watched this man weep as the Holy Spirit moved in our church services, and with his tears seemed to be much heartache and pain; I often wondered what his past held, and what heavy load he carried. Usually, when I give the invitation for people to come forward to receive prayer, Bruce would sit in his seat, tears rolling down his cheeks, with what appeared as a thousand pound weight in the expression on his face. It is the same weight that kept him pressed to his seat for so long, and prevented him from coming forward for prayer.

One Tuesday I gave the invitation, and to my amazement Bruce rose from his seat and walked toward me. I smiled at him and asked, "Bruce, how can I pray for you tonight? I see you with so much sadness, and I believe that God will help you, if you ask him to." With moist red eyes he looked at me and said, "Miss Candy, you don't know much about me, but when I was a young man, I joined the military to protect and serve my country. I was good with a rifle, so I was trained as a gunner. The Bible says, 'Thou shalt not kill' and I have killed so many people . . . too many . . . and God will never forgive me—I can't even forgive myself. I drink to ease my pain, and to try to forget their faces."

Now the tears that were flowing weren't only Bruce's tears, they were mine as well. I searched for words to say, but sometimes there are no words. I find that just the act of listening and being a friend is sometimes all that is needed. There we stood, two friends weeping, then lifting our tears upward to God in prayer.

I know that God heard our prayers, and I know he loves this man who doesn't love himself. I know that I love him. I believe that God uses our hearts to fill us with his love, because he wants to embrace ones like this. Because he committed acts too horrible for his mind to accept, Bruce has rejected himself and taken on a lifestyle that society rejects, that reinforces what he feels about himself. The good news is that "the one who comes to Me I will by no means cast out" (John 6:37). There are no outcasts, no . . . *Orphans of God*.

True Confessions

My husband, Kent Christmas, has been a pillar in The Bridge Ministry since we began, and he often speaks under the bridge to the homeless. One evening after he had finished preaching, a man came to him and asked, "Are you a priest?" Kent said, "No, I am a pastor, but I am willing to help you however I can." The man replied, "I was hoping you were a priest because I need someone to hear my confessions. Will you hear them?" My husband told him that God would hear his confessions, and that he would pray with him as he repented.

Kent led him to a more private location, away from the noise of the church service. Softly the homeless man began to speak: "Eight years ago, I murdered a man," he confessed, as his voice began to break and tears trickled down his cheeks. "When I was younger, I raped my sister. I live in torment from my past and need absolution. I need forgiveness! Can you forgive me?"

Moved with compassion, Kent prayed with him, and assured him of God's Word: "If we confess our sins, He is faithful and just to forgive us our sins and to cleanse us from all unrighteousness" (1 John 1:9). He prayed with him, and the homeless man disappeared into the darkness.

I have to believe that God has a special grace for people who have lost their way, who drink to forget, who can't forgive themselves. The reason I believe this is because God continues to "call" people like me to go reach for lost sheep like these. In God's eyes, sin is sin, no great or small. Jesus didn't take small stripes for small sin, and large stripes for big sins. He died for all sin; all sin must come under his blood to be forgiven. That includes my sin, your sin, and the sin of the depraved. "For all have sinned and fall short of the glory of God, and are justified freely by his grace through the redemption that came by Christ Jesus" (Rom. 3:23-24, NIV).

Grace is synonymous with loving kindness, good will, benefit, or divine favor; it is "not of works, lest any man should boast" (Eph. 2:9,

KJV), but a simple gift. Where sin abounds, grace much more abounds, and although the homeless may look to some like wretches and sinners, Jesus, I believe, sees them through his tender, gracious eyes, not as orphans, but children of God.

Craig Thomas's Story

My name is Craig Thomas and I am a follower of Jesus Christ. I am also recovering from a drug addiction. I was born forty eight years ago just outside of Chicago. My dad was a hardworking man and my mom stayed at home to care for me, my two older brothers, and two younger sisters. My parents believed in going to church. They had us there every Sunday morning, Sunday evening, Wednesday night, every crusade, Vacation Bible School, and even summer camp.

Needless to say, growing up I learned a little bit about the Lord. I believed in God the Father, God the Son, and God the Holy Spirit, but as a thirteen-year-old boy the world's ways seemed more exciting to me. I loved the girls, and I liked the way beer made me feel, and smoking pot was even better. After graduating from high school, I went to a trade school in Dayton, where I became a certified structural welder. From there I moved to Houston, Texas, where I worked on the oil rigs out of Galveston. My partying continued to increase throughout high school and trade school. After I took the job in Houston, my partying increased even more until it became a daily part of my life. There wasn't anything I wouldn't try.

Eventually I made the decision to move back to the Chicago area to marry my high school sweetheart. She was the woman of my dreams and I wanted to spend my life with her. We married and I began work at US Steel. We had two boys and accumulated a lot of things during our thirteen years together. My wife enjoyed social drinking but no drugs. I was quite different. I drank, smoked pot, and snorted cocaine daily. She didn't seem to care that I was not around much. Since she lived in a beautiful house, had money in the bank, a wallet full of credit cards, and was able to take vacations most people only dream about, she never complained much.

Then an event took place which would make things turn worse. I was at work one night and caught a guy in the bathroom shooting cocaine into his arm. I thought at first that he was crazy, but another part of me wanted to try it just once. It was the worst mistake I ever made. I loved the feeling so much I couldn't stop. It became all I cared and thought about. I started missing work and would sometimes not go home for days at a time. I went through our savings account, checking account, took out loans, sold my boat, sold my motorcycle, and stopped going to work. I was devastated. I could not believe how this drug took total control of my life. I gave up. I could not hurt my family or job anymore so I walked away from both and lived out of hotels or my car, at least until the money ran out. It was then I rounded up some girls to work as prostitutes at the truck stops. I stole cars and semis, ran drugs and guns, and did just about anything to supply my drug habit. After a period of time it became so tough I had to leave town. I left and bounced from city to city, just surviving. I felt the Lord calling me, but I never stuck around anywhere too long. He works in such loving, caring ways that I was starting to notice. There were several times he sent people to tell me he loved me. Then they would pray for me and I would feel his presence. I would always just pull away.

While living in a motel, working in Nashville, being paid on Friday, being broke on Sunday, having to eat at the mission or churches or soup kitchens to make it until the next payday just to do it all over again, I was broken inside. I had been living like this for more years than I care to remember, but on August 23, 2009, that would all change. It was a Tuesday and time for supper under the Jefferson Street Bridge where Candy Christmas serves food. I went every Tuesday, but this time was different. When I arrived at the service under the bridge, I felt the Lord pulling on my heart to call upon him and this time I didn't pull away. I fell to my knees, totally broken. It took thirty-five years, but I finally surrendered to him. I cried out to him, "Help me, please. I know

I'm yours. Take all of me and show me the way. I can't live this way anymore." I once again felt His presence.

That evening, the guest speaker at The Bridge Ministry was Candy's friend, Pastor Josh Hannah. He spoke on hope. After the service, I approached Candy and told her that I needed the hope that Pastor Hannah was telling us about. She then told me about the HOPE Center, which is a drug rehabilitation center offered by Pastor Hannah's church. I had never heard of Waverly, Tennessee or a HOPE Center, but I knew that they were there for me. I left with them that night, and they took me to the place where my hope was restored. God made things happen so fast after my prayer, and I knew it was him. I felt the peace that passes all understanding. It is something you can't really explain in words but can only feel inside your heart.

Since that day, I've never looked back. God created me, Jesus died for me, and the Holy Spirit leads me through each day. I know how real God really is. I will never turn my back on him again. I have been changed as a result of Candy being obedient to the Lord's calling, and serving under the bridge to folks like me every Tuesday night. My heart is now full of gladness and joy!

Chapter Three

Since I Laid My Burdens Down

Prelude

In 1 Peter we find the words, "casting all your care upon him, for he cares for you" (5:7). I find that in my walk with God, the "casting of the cares" is relatively easy. When I go to the Lord in my daily devotion, I usually present a very large catalog of cares. I've made my list and checked it twice of all the things that I need for him to do for me that day.

The trouble that I usually have is in the "he cares for you." For many years I read that scripture assuming that Peter is reassuring us of Christ's affection for us. I have come to see that Peter was saying that if we submit to God and resist the devil (the previous verse), then we can cast our cares on him and he will "care" on our behalf. The problem becomes God's and not ours. So in a sense we can say, "I don't care!" We no longer are in turmoil, because we have turned our situation over to God and he is in control. The sign of faith in the life of a believer is walking through life in peace through faith in God's Word.

In Mark 4 Jesus begins to tell the parable of the sower: "And these are they which are sown among thorns; such as hear the word, and the cares of this world and the deceitfulness of riches, and the lusts of other things entering in, choke the word, and it becomes unfruitful" (Mark 4:18-19, KJV). The sower goes out to plant the Word of God and some seed falls by the way, some on stony ground, and some among thorns. The thorns grew and choked it, and it yielded no fruit. This thorny ground that Jesus was talking about was the cares of life. Some translations actually say "worries." Worry and the "cares of life" negate the faith we received from hearing God's Word.

In the time of the prophet Daniel, King Nebuchadnezzar had made a decree that everyone must bow and worship his golden idol. Anyone who did not obey this law would be cast into a furnace and incinerated. Shadrach, Meshach, and Abednego had put their trust in the Lord, and when everyone else bowed, they did not. "Oh, Nebuchadnezzar, we are not *care*ful to answer you in this matter." Here the three Hebrew children are standing before an angry king. They are about to be thrown into a furnace that is now seven times hotter than it originally was. It seems that if there was ever a time to be worried, now is the time. Their answer was, "We don't *care*! If we go into the furnace, God is able to deliver us. But if he doesn't, we still will not bow!" Their hearts were at rest in their faith in God. (See Daniel 3 for the full story.)

"*Casting* all your care on him . . . ." This word "casting" in the original Greek is the word *epiripto* which means to hurl, or throw in a sudden motion, or "in haste, throw upon," much like you would hurl a load onto the back of a beast of burden (*Strong's* 1977). The only other place this word is used is Luke 19:35, "and they cast their garments upon the colt, and they set Jesus thereon" (KJV), speaking of Jesus triumphal entry into Jerusalem.

Many times I have been south of the California and Texas border where little donkeys are frequently used to carry heavy burdens. I've seen those small creatures carry loads as high as they are tall, and their legs seemed to bow under the weight. They obediently carry their master's burdens for miles, in the heat down long dusty roads, or up steep hills. My heart goes out to them because of the heavy load they carry. The truth of the matter is that if the master had no "beast of burden" he would be carrying his "burden" himself. Many times we carry our burdens needlessly. Peter was telling us that we no longer need to carry our burdens, but we can hurl all our care upon Jesus and he will carry it for us.

I once heard a story about a weary traveler who was walking down a country road carrying a large burden. A man driving an old farm truck saw him and pulled to the shoulder and motioned to the traveler to hop on the back. After some time, the man driving the truck looked in his rear view mirror to check on his passenger. Much to his surprise, the traveler was sitting comfortably on the truck bed, yet still carrying his heavy parcel on his back. He turned to the man and smiling kindly said, "Why don't you lay your burden down and let it ride?"

Many times, I have gone to the Lord heavy hearted, seemingly carrying the weight of the world on my shoulders. I have poured out my troubles to him literally hurling the weight of them upon him. Immediately as I have begun casting, He began carrying. Even though my circumstances had not changed, the one carrying the weight of the load had shifted. I have begun to take the attitude that "I don't care." Not that things are not important to me anymore, or that I am flippant. I am simply learning to allow Jesus to care on my behalf, to care "for" me. To begin to *Lay my burden down*, and let it ride."

Pop-Tarts and Coats

Long before my family sang gospel music, my dad pastored a small church, so I was born into a pastor's home. I was raised in church, and have known a walk with the Lord most of my life. Like many Christians I think, I have a hard time translating the verses we read in the pages of the Bible to actual, everyday living. I guess what I am trying to say is, I can quote Bible verses like "ask, and ye shall receive" (John 16:24, KJV) and "What things soever ye desire, when ye pray, believe that ye receive them, and ye shall have them" (Mark 11:24 , KJV), but I never really took God at his Word. My walk with the Lord was in my own strength, getting things done with my own talents and abilities, never allowing God to be my source.

One thing that I have come to understand about working with the poor is that when you pray about needs, God will answer very quickly. I believe he wants us to depend completely upon him. "Is not this the

The homeless receiving a hot meal

fast that I have chosen ... to deal thy bread to the hungry ... [to] bring the poor that are cast out [the homeless] to thy house? when thou seest the naked, that thou cover him .... Then shalt thou call, and the LORD shall answer; thou shalt cry, and he shall say, Here I am." (Isa. 58:6-9, KJV)

In the infant stages of my work under the bridge, my days were consumed with buying and storing non-perishable food items, purchasing and sorting socks and underwear, going to Goodwill to find used clothing, all to distribute to the homeless in the coming weeks. This newfound love was what woke me in the mornings and what

I thought of all day. I was so involved in the day-to-day that I hadn't looked ahead to the upcoming change of seasons, and the cold-front that was fast approaching.

Living here in Nashville, I've noticed that seasons change very quickly. The weather can take a sudden turn. One moment you may be enjoying eighty-five degree temperatures, and over night the weather may drop forty degrees. Almost instantly you can find yourself unprepared. This particular year, the weather took a drastic turn on a Tuesday night as we were having church under the bridge. We had fed a couple hundred people that night, but as the service went on I could see my homeless friends pulling their arms out of their T-shirts and putting them down inside their shirts to keep warm. They were sitting there quietly, respectful of the Word of God being preached, but they were miserably cold and shivering. The reality suddenly hit me: "I didn't prepare for cold weather." I had not bought one long-sleeved shirt; I had no coat, no blanket, nothing! As soon as church ended, we began the grocery and clothing distribution. I was inundated with requests for any item we might have to keep them warm, and I was heartbroken.

I got into my car, turned the heat on high, went home to my warm home, crawled into my bed under my electric blanket, and I was miserable. I slept very little that night, and finally climbed out of bed before daylight. My heart was heavy, and in times like this all I know to do is find a quiet place to pray and tell my Father all about it. I began to pray and weep before the Lord in the darkness of the twilight of the morning. My weeping turned to sobs, as I could see the faces of my homeless friends pleading to me for warm clothing. In my mind's eye I could imagine them struggling through the night, trying to find warmth. I found myself lying out on the floor, crying to the Lord, until my tears fell on the carpet beneath me saying, "Lord! I have *got* to have coats."

I began to calculate. I decided that I could call churches around the country, whose pastors I am acquainted with. I could ask them to announce to their congregations that if anyone had an old coat in the back of their closet they didn't use, would they donate it to the homeless. However, I realized that these pastors would not be able to make the announcement until Sunday, which meant that I would not see coats begin to trickle in for approximately a month. But today is Wednesday and my friends are cold today. I continued to pray.

After some time, I felt a huge sigh rise up inside me. I took a deep breath and I lay there in the darkness, feeling peace. I could no longer pray; somehow I had the assurance that God had heard me and that everything would be all right. I began to start my morning. I did a few chores around my home; I got my children up for school and fed them their breakfast, and began to dress to go into the office. My cell phone rang, and as I looked at the caller ID, I noticed that it was a friend of mine whom I'd gotten Pop-Tarts from on a couple of occasions, so I said "Hello." The voice on the other end of the line asked, "Hey! You don't need any coats, do you?" A little startled, I replied, "Why, yes I do! How many do you have, and how much do they cost?" He answered,

"I have a pallet of coats, and they are free! Do you have a warehouse where I could back a semi-truck up and unload?" "How long will it take you to get here?" I asked. "Two hours," was his reply. "I'll get the warehouse, you bring the coats!" and I hung up the phone.

I had two prayers answered at once. I had been praying for a warehouse, but I had been afraid to take the step of faith to sign a lease. God gave me the faith for the warehouse, and then he filled it—all in one prayer.

When the truck arrived, there were over five hundred coats inside. I had seen a miracle! My husband and I loaded the little box truck full of coats and headed to the bridge. We had such a wonderful time giving away coats that night and the homeless were extremely grateful.

The disciples "said to the Lord, 'Increase our faith!'" (Luke 17:5). I find it interesting that Jesus never began giving them faith exercises; he merely began to tell them to use their small faith. If you have faith "the size of a mustard seed" then you can see your prayers answered, and the impossible become possible. At that moment, I realized that when I stopped doing things in my own strength and began to depend completely on the Lord as my source, I could *Lay my burdens down.*

Blessings from Hurricane Katrina

The success of The Bridge Ministry's Tuesday night outreach confirmed to me that my mission in life was to feed the poor. I was reminded of when Jesus said, "Follow me, and I will make you fishers of men" (Matt. 4:19, KJV). Being raised in Louisiana, I was taught to fish

Candy Christmas prays a blessing for our homeless friends

about the time I learned to walk. I never went fishing without a worm on the hook to draw the fish to my line. If I wanted to win souls, then I would use bait. Not wanting to leave anyone in need out, I began to open feeding programs all over the city. The Jefferson Street outreach helped me realize that if we provided a hot meal, we could draw a crowd, thus being able to share the gospel with many souls, hopefully winning them to Christ. We would serve the hot meal first (I could never present the gospel to hungry people) and distribute free, numbered tickets. We could then retain our crowd throughout the church service with the promise of a raffle for sleeping bags and a bicycle. Then we would distribute truckloads of clothing and grocery items that we had acquired from the local food bank. My thinking has always been, and still is, give them so much that they have to have help carrying it away. Then they will invite their family members and friends to come help them carry it, and we'll win their souls, too. I have asked the Lord to let me win a million souls for Christ in my lifetime. I truly believe that this is the method he has given me to do it.

I felt God wanting me to reach out to the four corners of Nashville, so the first feeding program we began apart from the Jefferson Street Bridge was in a parking lot on Shelby Avenue, situated in the middle of several lower income housing projects in Nashville's east side. The second program was on the north side in Gallatin, and the third on Murfreesboro Road on the south side. Each program was hosted by a local congregation in that area of town, as well as a core group of my regular volunteers who were with me every Tuesday under the bridge as well. As you can imagine, we became exhausted. The precious volunteers that God has sent me have a heart to serve and, most of all, a heart to win souls.

As the word of the outreach got out, we began receiving and accepting invitations from other inner city ministries to sing, minister the Word, and distribute goods and food to the poor. One particular night we were invited to minister at a local mission on the west side. I had arranged for my driver to load the box truck full of goods, and all the volunteers were to go with me to help pray with people and lead them to Jesus. There was one small problem: we had no supplies. The warehouse was empty. I was spent financially and emotionally, and left with no money even to buy the things I had promised the people at the mission.

I had been reading a book written by a man who asked God to surprise him. Each day, this man would journal the surprises he came upon whether big or small. God began to challenge me to believe him to meet needs that were beyond my own abilities. The writer of Ephesians says, "Now to Him who is able to do exceedingly abundantly above all that we ask or think" (3:20). My mind was clouded with sheer panic and my emotions were raw. I didn't know what else to do but pray, "Lord, surprise me!" I began to pace the floor calling on God. I wept. I pleaded. I knelt, stood, then paced more, desperate for an answer from God. I knew so many people were depending on me, and furthermore, I had given my word.

My brothers are very successful businessmen in Nashville; they own a fleet of buses that they lease to various musical artists, movie stars, and even corporations who need to travel. This was the time just after Hurricane Katrina in New Orleans, and much aid was being sent south. A large corporation had leased several buses from my brothers to carry supplies to Katrina victims, and the tour was now over. The bus had been returned to my brothers' lot still loaded with much of their supplies. My brothers have always been mindful of The Bridge Ministry, so they contacted the leaser who said, "We no longer have need of it. Do with it what you want." I was completely unaware that my brothers had asked some of their employees to deliver all the supplies to my front porch. Little did I know that the entire time I was praying and pleading with God for the answer, the answer was already sitting on my front porch! I stepped outside to get the mail and almost stumbled over it.

Still exhausted, I looked at all this "stuff" and didn't see a miracle. The supplies that God had provided were things that I wouldn't normally take to the outreaches. I was accustomed to distributing things like socks, underwear, T-shirts, sleeping bags, and food. What I now had were towels, washclothes, toothbrushes, laundry detergent, and a vast array of hygiene products. In my mind, my prayers weren't answered at all. I had never given homeless people laundry detergent. What was God thinking? I looked to the heavens and audibly told the Lord, "This isn't what I asked for, but if this is what you sent, I guess it will have to do."

Evening came and we arrived at the mission. To my great surprise, all of these recovering addicts and alcoholics lived in an old motel that had been converted into a mission. They lived there, but it was their responsibility to provide their own toiletries, towels, etc. The things that they so desperately needed were exactly the things we had brought. God knew what they needed much more than I did. If someone had given me the money to buy supplies for that event, I would not have bought one thing that we had taken. Over and over God has taught me to depend completely on him for everything. I am very headstrong, and this has been a hard lesson for me to learn. Still many times, I still have to be reminded to . . . *lay my burden down.*

Chapter Four

Climbing Up the Mountain

Prelude

"Take now your son, your only son Isaac, whom you love, and go to the land of Moriah, and offer him there as a burnt offering on one of the mountains of which I shall tell you."

Genesis 22:2

Nowadays reality shows are very popular on television. I think the general public has become somewhat bored with the humdrum of scripted shows and have opted for something a little more thrilling. Maybe subconsciously we're all sitting there living vicariously through the participants, looking for something a little more exciting in life for ourselves. Most weekends our kids hang out at our house, and they usually bring all of their friends with them. We like to gather around the television and watch those survivor guys who scale the mountains with no security ropes. They eat live reptiles and rodents, and live in conditions that don't seem humanly possible. They perform death-defying acts that give me a head rush just watching them from my sofa. Most of these programs have a disclaimer at the bottom of the screen that reads, "These stunts are performed by trained profession-als. Please don't try this at home."

I feel that the next story that you are about to read should come with just such a disclaimer (except for the trained professionals part). In our intense desire to know God, Kent and I have taken risks and steps of faith that I wouldn't recommend to anyone else, unless they knew for certain that they were prompted by the Holy Spirit to do so. At times I think we have walked the high wire without a net, and I wonder if the Lord, at times, bailed us out merely because he winked at our ignorance. He might have thought, "I'd better go rescue Kent and Candy before they seriously hurt themselves!" In any case, he has proven himself faithful to us. So here goes . . .

Several years ago, Kent and I felt challenged as we read Malachi 3:10, "prove me now herewith, saith the LORD of hosts, if I will not open you the windows of heaven, and pour you out a blessing, that there shall not be room enough to receive it" (KJV). We've never been much on the prosperity doctrine, but after much prayer consideration we decided that for a season we would increase our giving. We de-cided to give to God half of our gross income. We were by no means wealthy—actually at that time we were struggling to make ends meet.

Most of the time there was just enough money to pay our bills and eat out in restaurants occasionally. Giving half of our income to the church would be a sacrifice for us, but God had given us grace for our journey, "come what may." When others around us saw us beginning to barely scrape by, they tried to dissuade us from our commitment. Some onlookers even became frustrated, viewing our lack as senseless and silly. Undaunted, we happily ate our beans and rice, feeling that we were doing what God had asked of us.

At one point we fell so far behind in our mortgage payment that we were only a couple of weeks away from foreclosure proceedings. The strain on us, I admit, was at times indescribable. We had fallen behind on payments to all of our creditors, and it became a continuous battle to keep our heads above water. We had worked hard and had earned enough money to catch up on our house note. As it turned out, the money that we had earned was also the same amount that we had calculated would make us current in our giving commitment as well. Kent and I had a decision to make. Do we pay the mortgage or do we give to God? We earnestly sought the Lord together in prayer for the answer, and we both decided that we would give to the Lord.

We had been studying the life of Abraham, the father of the faithful. We had many discussions between us about how he had not staggered at the promises of God, how he maintained a strong faith that enabled him to offer Isaac. We were not by any means asked to offer anything so great as a son, but in our hearts we were raising the knife to all that we owned. We understood that it wasn't money God was wanting from us, but our obedience, our willingness to do all he had asked us to do, whatever the cost.

We sat together at our kitchen table, and Kent wrote the check to our home church for the full amount and said, "Lord, today we give you our Isaac. We offer you our home, our credit rating, and all that we have we give to you." Within days of this step of faith, there was a dramatic turn in our situation, and we received an unexpected windfall. It was enough money for us to pay our bills, and mortgage, with some left over. Finally the stress was lifted off of us, and the sun was shining again. It felt so good to breathe without feeling the weight of the world on our shoulders. After eighteen months, we were released from our commitment, and resumed our normal giving.

We believed that we had passed the test and that instantly our lives we would different. We thought the windows of heaven would immediately be opened, and that blessing would overtake us. Toward the end of this season in our lives, I found out that we were expecting our son, Nicholas. While traveling from Nashville to California to fulfill a ministry obligation, I suddenly went into premature labor and gave birth to him at twenty-seven weeks of gestation. Because of our lack of income, we had discontinued our health insurance. Now instead of anticipating great blessing coming our way, it seemed we were facing financial ruin. The hospital administrator at Oakland Children's Hospital told us that the projected cost of Nicholas's hospital stay, if in fact he lived, would be three quarters of a million dollars! All of a sudden it seemed that our faith had been in vain. Our fear said, "See, because you gave to God all those months, when you should have been paying for health insurance, you will lose everything, including your baby boy!"

The day of Nicholas' birth was grim. Our son's life was in grave jeopardy, we were 2,500 miles from our home and family, and our faith was shaken to its foundation. Our lives were spinning out of control, as uncertainty and confusion swirled around us. Kent and I clung to each other like children in a hurricane, knowing that our only hope was in the Lord.

I was immediately placed on a gurney and rushed out of the emergency room to be prepped for surgery. Kent stepped into the hallway of the hospital, trying to find a quiet place to collect his thoughts and to pray. The Spirit of the Lord sweetly reminded him of the day that we sat at our kitchen table, offering everything we owned to him. God spoke to his heart and said, "Because you gave me your Isaac that day, I am giving you the life of your son. Everything will be alright."

Nicholas weighed two pounds and stayed in ICU nearly three months. He never required any type of surgery, and every day until his release he grew healthier and gained strength. Much to our amazement, news of our dilemma traveled across the country and many friends began sending cards filled with well wishes—and donations. People that we had never met heard about us and began praying for us and sending financial help. This outpouring of love was a much-needed balm to our battle-weary souls. Our son continued to thrive, and we watched as the Lord opened the windows of heaven and miraculously paid every medical bill that we incurred. God had provided, just as he had promised.

Abraham had waited patiently many years for the promise of God to be fulfilled in his life. God had given him wealth and property, but the one desire of Abraham's heart that had yet to be granted was that of an heir. Twenty-five years passed from the promise to the birth of Isaac. Yet after the promise was delivered, Abraham was told to offer him as a burnt offering. Abraham's trust in the Lord was mind-boggling. We never read a discourse between Abraham and God where he tries to change God's mind or where he offers to take Ishmael up the mountain instead. Abraham immediately obeyed, beginning his journey the very next morning, no questions asked.

Imagine the ache in Abraham's heart as he began preparing for the journey. Maybe Sarah comes to him a little confused about it. "Where are you going?" she asks. "I'm climbing up the mountain, I'm going to offer a burnt sacrifice to God," he answers. "Why are you taking Isaac? I need him to stay here, I have things for him to do." She bargains. "Do you want me to have him catch a ram for you? Where is your sacrifice?"

Surely Abraham wondered how could he tell Sarah, "I'm going to offer our only son." How could he find words to explain God's request to the child's mother? It was one thing for him to believe that after Isaac is dead God would raise him up. It is altogether another to ask others to share in your convictions at such a great risk as losing your only child.

Along my own journey of faith, I have learned that it is not always prudent to share with others the dealings of God in our lives. When he asks things of us, he will equip us with a certain grace to walk them out. Friends who are on the outside looking in are not walking in that same grace. Often well wishers will try to discourage us from personal sacrifices merely because they don't understand.

Jesus began to tell his disciples that he must go to Jerusalem to suffer and die. Peter loved Jesus, and recognized him as Lord and could not comprehend that it could be the will of the Father that Jesus would be crucified. Peter took Jesus aside and said, "'Far be it from You, Lord; this shall not happen to You!' But He turned and said to Peter, 'Get behind Me, Satan! You are an offense to Me, for you are not mindful of the things of God, but the things of men'" (Matt. 16:22-23).

Abraham's three-day journey only prolonged the inevitable, and multiplied his grief and pain. It's possible to assume that Isaac innocently chattered along the journey, as children often do, making plans for the future: "You know Dad, when we get back home, let's get started building that barn you and I talked about." Or maybe he said something like, "When I have a son, I want to take him up the mountain to worship God just like this, Dad." Without his faith faltering, Abraham continued climbing up the mountain.

Isaac carried the wood for the altar for which he would be offered upon. When they reached their destination he said, "My father, I see the fire and the wood, but where is the lamb for the burnt offering?" His father answered, "My son, God will provide Himself a lamb." Abraham began to prophesy, as if the heavens opened momentarily to allow him to see into the future. He spoke of a time when on that same mountain, Moriah, another son of promise would be offered as a sacrifice.

With the altar built, Isaac willfully lay down upon it, bound and trusting his father. Abraham raised his knife to slay his only son when the voice of the angel of the Lord called out to stop him: "Abraham, lay not your hand upon the lad, neither do him no harm, now I know that you fear God, you have not withheld your son, your only son." Abraham had passed the test, and not far away he saw a ram caught in the thickets. God had provided just as he had promised.

Many years later Jesus Christ climbed up a mountain, a hill called Golgotha in Moriah, carrying a wooden cross. God the Father would offer his own son, the only begotten, for the sins of humankind. Jesus willfully lay upon the cross, trusting his Father. There would be no ram in the thickets, no voice calling it to a halt. The son of promise, heaven's darling, the lamb of God, would suffer a cruel death. God had provided, just as he had promised: "Surely he hath borne our grief and carried our sorrows: yet we did esteem him stricken, smitten of God, and afflicted. But he was wounded for our transgressions, he was bruised for our iniquities: the chastisement of our peace was upon him; and with his stripes we are healed" (Isa. 53:4-5, KJV).

Often when our faith is tested, the things that we go through may not seem spiritual. We wonder how God can use this for his glory and purpose in our lives. It's the times when we go through lack or reversal that our faith goes from being merely words on a page of the Bible

(L-R) Nicholas Christmas, Jasmine Brady Christmas &
JonMichael Brady under the bridge

to become our inner strength and lifeline to survival. This is no reality television show; this is real life. Don't give up, keep pressing on . . . *Climbing up the Mountain!*

The Health Department

One Tuesday night in 2008, we loaded the trucks with the hot food we had prepared for the homeless, along with the usual grocery bags and toiletry items, and headed down to the bridge. We gathered around in prayer for the service, and each volunteer then went to their post, singing, welcoming, and serving. The homeless lined up all the way down to the river for what possibly was the only hot meal they would eat all week, and we gladly served them.

Almost as soon as we started the service, a woman, flanked by police, approached me and said, "Excuse me, ma'am. I am with the Tennessee Department of Health and by law you are required to have a permit for serving hot meals to the public. Can I see that permit?" My face instantly became flushed because I knew that we didn't have what she was looking for, but the homeless needed to eat, and if she shut us down, I knew that wouldn't be happening that night. I replied to her with a bit of anxiety, "I am sorry, but we don't have a permit. We are a non-profit organization with a heart for the poor, and the only street ministry that feeds these people." "Ma'am, you can't serve food to the public without a permit," the woman said, "so tonight I am going to have to shut you down."

My heart sank into what seemed like my stomach, and I tried to think quickly. I called one of the volunteers over to me and explained the situation. I sent her and a few others back to the warehouse to gather all the packaged food we could find, and bring it back to the bridge as soon as they could, so the homeless wouldn't leave hungry. They left in a flash, and I walked back to the serving line to announce the heavy news.

That night when I got home, all I could think of was the events that had transpired that night. One of the Health Department policies was that all food served to the public had to be prepared in a commercial kitchen or served out of a mobile kitchen, neither of which we had the money for. I had no idea how we would meet this requirement by next Tuesday, so I went to my Father who knows all the answers, and wept on my knees until I felt peace.

The next morning I was on a mission. My first call was to a local non-profit organization that we frequented; I asked if they had mobile kitchens or could help me find one. They informed me that they had one they had been trying to donate to other ministries for the last several months to no avail, and transferred me to the person who could help. I just knew this was the Lord answering my prayers. The Bridge Ministry didn't have the money in the account for a mobile kitchen, but here God was opening the door for it to be donated to us and I couldn't have been more ecstatic. When the woman in charge of the mobile kitchen picked up the phone, I explained to her our situation, of how we needed a mobile kitchen, and how we were interested in receiving the one they were trying to donate. The lady quickly informed me that they would not be donating the kitchen to our ministry, but that we could purchase it from them for $7,000 if we wanted it. Disappointed and a bit hurt, I told the woman we would pass on their kitchen and hung up the phone. I didn't understand why this organization would try to donate the mobile kitchen to other ministries, but when we needed it, they put a large price tag on it. When you are a small ministry, or a small anything for that matter, it's easy to be taken advantage of, but humility and a soft answer, however hard, is Jesus' way.

As I continued to make calls about a mobile kitchen, I was surprised to hear that the local news media had picked up our story and was advocating our cause to the city. They interviewed a homeless man, who said, "It isn't right that the health department shut down good people who feed me the only hot meal I eat all week. If I don't get to eat the food they give me, then I have to eat out of garbage bins and dumpsters. So in the end, it doesn't matter if these people's food is inspected or not, because it is better than my alternative." This sweet man's statement created a large outcry in the city against the Health Department, and gave me even more vigor to fight our battle.

I found a mobile kitchen that I decided to step out in faith and buy for the ministry, but when I went to make the purchase, The Bridge Ministry volunteers stepped in and bought it so that the ministry didn't pay a dime. Let me say here that our volunteers are some of the best people on earth, not just for buying a mobile kitchen, but for the hours they spend each week without pay in a warehouse and under a bridge faithfully serving the homeless. Without them, this ministry wouldn't run, and I am forever indebted to them for their hard work and willingness to serve. When the next Tuesday came, we pulled up under the bridge in our new mobile kitchen, and we were on our way to receiving a permit from the Health Department. Of course, the Health Department came back to inspect our progress, and cleared us to continue serving food to the homeless.

A year had passed, and our mobile kitchen was serving us well Tuesday after Tuesday. One day my phone rang and it was the same non-profit organization who had tried to sell us their mobile kitchen. The woman on the other end said, "Mrs. Christmas, I am calling in regards to the mobile kitchen you had inquired about a year ago. I wanted to let you know that we still have it and were wondering if you were still interested?" "Well, we went ahead and obtained a mobile kitchen from another source, and aren't looking to purchase another one at this point," I told her. She replied," I know that the original price was $7,000, but we'll take your best offer." "$1,500 is all I can do," I explained. "Done. When can you pick it up?" she replied. As I was talking with this woman, one of our volunteers, who had overheard the conversation, stepped into my office and said, "Don't worry about the money. I want to pay for the kitchen as a donation to the ministry." And with that the Lord had answered our prayers with two mobile kitchens that we never paid a dime for.

Since we have begun The Bridge Ministry, it has been nothing but a learning process, and still continues to be every day. I learn more about the Lord, myself, the homeless, the volunteers, and how to do things better. Part of our problem with the Health Department, as I stated before, was that we needed a permit or a certificate saying that we had taken and passed a class on food safety, and had passed an inspection of our facilities from the Health Department. Well we signed up, and about twelve of us took the class. We sat there for hours going over the right temperatures to cook food, proper food storage, and sanitary food preparation and handling. By the time the class was over, we were exhausted and ready for our certificate, when to my surprise, the man teaching us said, "Alright folks, that was a good class. Thanks for coming! You're dismissed." Now I'm a Southern girl from Louisiana with a little bit of pepper in me from time to time, and I marched up to him and began to protest, "Now wait a minute, the Health Department said we had to take this class to get a certificate. Well, I've taken the

Line at the mobile kitchen

class and I'm not leaving here until you give me my certificate." The man, puzzled, said, "Ma'am, I don't know who told you that you need a certificate, but you can go home. We have on record that you took the class, and that is enough." He persuaded me, so we went home empty handed and a little confused.

A few weeks later a friend of mine who works with the homeless commission inquired about the class and certificate, and when I told him what had happened he looked worried. He said, "Candy, I am sure you need that paper, in case they come down again wanting to see it, so you had better enroll in another class and make sure you get your certificate this time."

A bit perturbed, but wanting to do things the right way, two of the office staff at The Bridge Ministry enrolled in the class with strict instructions from me not to leave without a certificate of completion. When they returned, they told me a story that about knocked me to the ground. My daughter, Jasmine, who had gone, told me with sheer excitement, "Mom, you'll never believe what happened. When we went to the class, the instructor said the law had recently been changed and people who feed the homeless no longer have to serve out of commercial or mobile kitchens, and their facilities no longer need to be inspected by the health department. All they have to do is post an advisory saying the food being served has not been inspected and make sure they have a certificate saying they completed the Food Safety Class."

Astonished, I asked, "Are you sure that the law has been changed?" "Yes, Ma'am,". Jasmine replied, "I had the instructor call his supervisor and confirm. After his call he began to ask me what organization I was a part of and who I worked with. When I told him it was The Bridge Ministry, he asked if I knew Candy Christmas. He remembered how they had shut us down a while back. He said that the Health Department took so much flack for shutting us down that they changed the law so that we wouldn't have any more trouble. He concluded the conversation by saying he knew our volunteers had already been to the Food Safety Class and didn't get certificates, so he would make sure we got them in the next week straight from the state with our name on them."

I can't began to describe the shock and amazement I felt in hearing these words. The whole time that I was praying about the Health

Department, the mobile kitchen, and the voice inside saying we would get shut down for good, God was fighting the battles for me. I never prayed that the Lord would change the law because at that time I don't think I had the faith for that prayer. But Scripture says, "the effectual fervent prayer of a righteous man availeth much" (James 5:16b, KJV), and, "for with God all things are possible" (Mark 10:27b).

I believe that if we didn't have to work hard climbing to the top of the mountain, then finally reaching the mountain's peak wouldn't be nearly as rewarding. I have learned that I wouldn't know the Lord is truly the Lily of the Valley without having walked through a valley or two of my own, and that sometimes the parts of the journey that make you the person God needs you to be are the times when you're "climbing up the mountain."

Chapter Five

Jesus Built This Church on Love

Prelude

As I grow older, I realize that love isn't an emotion but a commitment. When I met my husband, Kent, it was his blue eyes that first attracted me. I had never seen such beautiful eyes, and when he focused them on me, it was if he looked into my soul.

As I got to know him better, I saw beyond the blue eyes and found that he was a man of prayer and outstanding character. These qualities were even more attractive to me than his outward appearance. I soon noticed that when I was in his presence my palms were sweaty, my heart would race, and I couldn't think of anything intelligent to say. The emotional euphoria that he incited in me made me realize that I wanted to be with him all the time, for the rest of my life.

After we were married and the newness of the relationship paled, the realities of life began to set in. As with most couples early in marriage, we struggled financially, and the day our first child was born, Kent was laid off his job. At that point the euphoria was pretty much out the window, and commitment came into play.

It is very sad to see so many young couples embrace the opinion that marriage is a lot like dating in high school: "If it doesn't work out, we'll divorce." The marriage vows that we recited at the altar say, "For richer or poorer, in sickness and in health, until death do us part." In this statement we verbalize a commitment before God and all who witness.

Jesus may have not taken this exact vow to us, his bride, but he proved his commitment by walking up Calvary and laying down his life. By his actions he plainly stated, "Until death do us part." In Ephesians 5:25 the love of Christ is likened to that of a husband, saying, "Husbands, love your wives, just as Christ also loved the church and gave Himself for her."

Not only have I made a vow of devotion to my husband, but to my children as well. Only such a commitment could cause a parent to override a tired body and stay awake to rock a fevered child through the night. Because of my love and obligation to nurture my child, I would not be anywhere else on the planet, than right there watching over my little one.

Every week there is one statement that I make to the congregation: "If no one has told you they love you today, let me be the first: I love you. Some visitors to The Bridge Ministry have been puzzled or even offended by this statement. "You should tell them Jesus loves them," I've heard some say. Week after week we proclaim the message of the love of Jesus and the mercy of the Father. I have found that many of the homeless feel abandoned by family and society, and look to us for affirmation and acceptance. When this statement is made to the homeless, it isn't empty words, but a pledge that assures them, rain, shine, sleet, or snow, you can count on us to be here. If you come to us sad, defeated, lonely, drunk, or high, we will be here, and you are still very much loved. On a regular basis, I will have them come to me and say, "I haven't been here in a while, I know you were worried about me," or "I know you were wondering where I've been; I was . . . ."

I really like the words written on the base of the Statue of Liberty: "Give me your tired, your poor, your huddled masses yearning to breathe . . . ." The United States of America made a pledge to the world that we would receive its outcasts who longed for freedom, and we stood by this promise by opening our harbors to immigrants from around the world. Somehow I can see these words etched near the foot of the cross, and in a sense they were: "Come to Me, all you who labor and are heavy laden, and I will give you rest" (Matt. 11:28). Then Jesus Christ proved his love and commitment to us by opening his arms to be nailed on a cross, for all of us seeking freedom from sin's bondage.

Jesus said that the greatest commandment is to love God, but the second is to "love your neighbor as yourself" (Mark 12: 28-31) . . . *Jesus Built This Church on Love.*

"Faith Works by Love"

Full Bellies, Full Heart

In the first year of The Bridge Ministry, I felt that it was important to get churches of all denominations in the community involved with our homeless outreach. Giving their members a place to use their gifts that might not have been used otherwise, and in turn, more of the homeless could be helped. I called the pastor of a local congregation, whom I knew very well, to come under the bridge and give his testimony to the homeless. He readily accepted the invitation. After the visit, he offered to send a bus the following Sunday to transport those among the homeless who would like to attend his church.

I was thrilled by his generous invitation and moved by his genuine love for the homeless. As I prayed throughout that week for the upcoming service, I began thinking about all the people I know who attend his church. I remembered people of notoriety and the affluent "upper-crust" who would be sitting in the congregation next to our sweet friends who are destitute. Knowing that there was no malice in the gesture, I still feared that they might be looked down on. I stewed and huffed around until I made up my mind that no one would look down on my friends. I would just dress them up—that's what I'd do. I was beside myself.

Being the mother hen that I am, I decided that I would gather some of the volunteers together that morning, and we would dress the homeless to look their best for Sunday school. I wanted them to

Faithful volunteers serving the Tuesday evening meal

walk in that church with their heads held high, instead of feeling out of place.

That cold Sunday morning that I had dreaded finally came. Kent and I and several of our volunteers loaded the box truck and hurried to the bridge. We had put the word out on the streets for all the homeless who were going to church that morning to meet us a little early, which they did. The truck was filled with hot coffee and breakfast as well as combs, baby wipes, new shirts and pants, and a new name-brand coat for everyone. Excitedly they began washing their faces and hands, and took turns dressing in their new clothes in the back of the box truck. By the time the church bus arrived, everyone was all shined up, with their stomachs full and looking like a million bucks! We all rode the bus together, laughing and talking and happy.

As we arrived at the church, we were greeted with an overwhelming outpouring of love. The members of the congregation were very friendly and welcoming. They had reserved a whole section towards the front of the sanctuary for us, and referred to the homeless as the "guests of honor." I realized immediately that my fears had been completely unfounded. I had needlessly expended my energy worrying, and we could have slept another hour longer that morning, as my husband so graciously pointed out.

I sat on the pew with my homeless friends, looking at row after row of them, looking at a sight that filled my heart with unspeakable joy. I felt like a proud mamma looking at the contented faces of her happy children and my face beamed with delight.

It was the first time in a long while that the homeless had been clean and warm and in a soft seat. With full bellies their eyes began to get heavy, and heads began to nod. If they had been looked down on that Sunday, they would not have known it. They looked like little children, row after row of them fast asleep.

Land of Misfit Toys

Approximately twenty-five years before he passed away, my grandfather purchased a cookie jar for my grandmother. It was very large and quite unusual, and for many years it sat on top of the refrigerator in their kitchen, big as life, for all who entered to see. It was a ceramic Peter Pan head with disproportionately big pointed ears, and the hat was the lid. The purchase of the cookie jar seemed to me very out of character for my grandfather, but nevertheless something about it struck his fancy, and it has now become a family heirloom. After my grandmother passed away I inherited it, and I have since become quite fond of it. Consequently I have now become a cookie jar collector and have now acquired many cookie jars in all shapes and sizes. They are all signed and numbered by my favorite designer, and I have them proudly displayed in my kitchen. One is in the shape of a large shoe, depicting "The Old Woman in the Shoe" nursery rhyme, and there are numerous intricately detailed children in all sizes mounted on it. Another is "Cinderella's Carriage" incrusted with faux jewels, accompanied with horses. But my favorite of the collection is "Noah's Ark" with all the animals hanging their heads out the windows. There is something about my cookie jars that makes me feel close to my grand-dad. I like admiring them and thinking of him. I have decided that if he fancied that big, old Peter Pan head, he would no doubt love my Noah's Ark.

Recently I was admiring one of the cookie jars, and I noticed that it was damaged. As I investigated further, I found others damaged as well. Beautiful Cinderella no longer has a nose, and one of "The Old Woman's" children has been decapitated. I began asking my family and anyone with access to our kitchen, if they knew what had happened to the cookie jars. Of course, no one would own up to any such knowl-edge, so I resigned myself to the fact that what's done is done. To any collector these flaws would render my cookie jars worthless, but I love them quite the same and would never consider parting with one, so nothing lost. My grandmother used to say, "Beauty is in the eye of the beholder," and they are still very beautiful to me, cracks and all.

I guess I made a bigger deal out of it than I had realized, because soon afterward I was surprised with a gift from my dear friend Shanda. She had heard about the whole ordeal. And wanting to console me, she bought me a huge ceramic rooster. It is fabulously ornate, stands more than two feet high, and is numbered and signed by my favor-ite cookie jar maker. I was so overwhelmed by her kind gesture that I wept. I brought it home and waited to take it out of the box until the house was empty of all my clumsy family members. I wasn't taking any chances with my perfectly pristine rooster. I gently remove the pack-ing and, carrying it with both hands, began slowly and deliberately climbing the stairs to the kitchen. Because of the rooster's size, our family dog lying on the top step was hidden from view. As I stepped up, I stepped onto him and he let out a loud yelp. I was startled, lost my balance, and went falling rooster first into the wall, breaking off his beautiful tail feathers. There I stood in disbelief, with the pieces of my beautiful rooster scattered all around.

I eased my way to a nearby chair and began wondering why it is that most of what I cherish in life is *broken*. My beloved Chihuahua, Max, climbed from a chair onto our pool table when he was four months old. Without warning he dove from it, landing on the floor and shattering all the tiny bones in his right shoulder. After hundreds of dollars and multiple surgeries, we have found that his impediment is irreparable. To some degree, he is *broken*.

When I met first met my husband, he had recently come out of a painful divorce. He was emotionally as well as financially devastated and starting all over again in his life. For a while he was homeless and at times slept in his car or on the floor in friend's homes. He was completely dependent on the kindness of others until he could regain his footing. During that time if he were to be asked, "How are you?" it would have been a struggle for him to choke back the tears. In a sense, he was *broken*.

Every year at Christmastime an animated television special airs that I have enjoyed watching since my childhood. It's the story of Rudolph the red-nosed reindeer who is shunned because of his red nose. My favorite part of the movie is when he runs away to a village called "The Land of Misfit Toys." There he finds refuge with a community of toys that were *broken* and cast aside. There was a Jack-in-the-Box who couldn't jump, a dolly that couldn't cry, a stuffed animal who had lost his stuffing. They were a diverse group, brought together by one commonality—*brokenness.* They had been rejected as acceptable Christmas gifts for children, but their impediment met the criteria for acceptance in the land of misfits. We might say that the one thing that made them outcasts also gave them acceptance. One toy wasn't too troubled by the imperfections of the other simply because they were acutely aware of their own flaws.

Do you ever wonder why Jesus chose the vocation of carpentry during his tenure upon this earth? Could it be that he knew that those whom he cherished most would be *broken*? Remember it was said of Jesus that he was sent to *heal the brokenhearted* (Luke 4:18). I can remember a time in my life when I was badly *broken,* and seemingly irreparable. I scooped up all the pieces of my shattered life as best I could and carried them, crying like a child, and laid them at the feet of my Father. Jesus, the Master Carpenter, lovingly began his work of restoration in my life. Much to my surprise, he never tried to reassemble all the pieces of my puzzle and glue them back together with all the cracks glaringly visible. I never felt the pounding of the Carpenter's hammer driving nails into my sides to reattach my parts. No, the Carpenter took the pounding of the nails in my place, and his sides were pierced for me. The Master Carpenter made a new creation out of this *broken* misfit.

Are you thinking what I'm thinking? I'm thinking that I might feel right at home among all my *broken* stuff, and I'm quite comfortable under a bridge with *broken* people. I'm thinking that I can overlook the flaws of my homeless friends because I'm acutely aware of my own. If the Master Carpenter made something new out of the mess I was in, he can surely do it for them too!

I have a sneaky feeling that if my granddad were alive and could see my cookie jars, he would admire them—even the *broken* ones. Because he spent his life preaching the gospel and loving people, I think he'd love my *broken* friends under the bridge too.

If you see Shanda, don't tell her I broke the rooster.

Chief's Story

Since we have been on the streets of Nashville, my husband and I have come to know a man who is quite a character with a very full personality. He rides a motorized wheelchair because one of his legs was amputated some time ago. For the last three or four years, he has carried a little fawn-colored Chihuahua on his knees and takes him everywhere he goes. Kent and I are dog lovers, especially the Chihuahua breed, and we found that this little Chihuahua is very misleading in his looks. His face is so adorable and small that on a couple of occasions Kent has made his way through the crowd to Chief's wheelchair to pet the dog. Instantly the little dog has shown his teeth and made a lunge for my husband, reminding him that he wasn't receptive to affection.

What love can do...

Kent has told me that he has noticed on Chief's own hands evidence of bite marks and scars from previous wounds.

Not long ago, Kent saw Chief under the bridge and made his way to the old man and his dog, this time keeping a safe distance. As he approached the two, the dog began to wag his tail as if he recognized Kent and was greeting him. Kent stepped in a little closer, and the Chihuahua leapt into Kent's arms and began to lick his face. Amazed at the drastic transformation of the dog's personality, Kent asked, "Chief, what's going on? What's happened?"

Chief smiled broadly and said, "That's what love can do. I rescued that little dog from a very abusive situation. He was severely beaten and mistreated, and he became ill tempered and came to trust no one. Every time I tried to feed him or reach my hand to him, he would bite me. I didn't care. I just kept loving him until finally he gave in and began to receive my love, and eventually loved me back. Now you see what love can do."

This dramatic transformation that took place right before our eyes in the life of a little dog amazed Kent and me. It took someone who recognized value in him, who could see beyond his rough exterior, and could love away the walls. I believe that God sends people like me, and countless others in the body of Christ, down to the street to see beyond rough exteriors and to love the unlovely. He sees value in the prostitutes, the addicts, and alcoholics. God loves them through us, and patiently loves away the walls.

This is the boundless, immeasurable love of God. While we were yet sinners, Christ saw value in us, so much so that he gave his life for us. I look at what I was and how God's love has transformed me, and I say, "That's what love can do." Jesus built this church on love . . . .

The Heart of a Star

"Love suffers long and is kind; love does not envy;
love does not parade itself, is not puffed up; does not behave
rudely, does not seek its own, is not provoked, thinks no evil; does
not rejoice in iniquity, but rejoices in the truth; bears all things,

believes all things, hopes all things, endures all things. Love never fails. . . . And now abide faith, hope, love, these three; but the greatest of these is love."

1 Corinthians 13:4-8a;13

When I was a teenager, I had the privilege of crossing paths a couple of times with a young girl about my age. I found her quite intriguing and extremely beautiful, and I was fascinated by her many unique qualities. Because we moved in different circles and because of the fact that she moved out of state to attend college, we lost touch with each other.

Several years later, she became an overnight success in the music industry, topping the charts in many genres and becoming the crème de le crème of Nashville's celebrated music artists. Over time I bought a few of her albums and remember many nights listening to her while traveling on concert tours with my family. I admired her from a distance.

Many years passed before I was to come in contact with her again. A mutual friend of ours had told her about "the church under the bridge" and had invited her to come sing for the homeless, which she did. Her appearance was not done as a favor to me, for she probably did not even realize my involvement until she arrived. She merely desired to help the poor, so she brought with her another non-profit organization that provided a new pair of shoes to every homeless person who attended that night. It was an outstanding night for the homeless—and for me as well since I was able to reconnect with an old friend.

That first night she visited the bridge was early fall, and the evening ended as quite a circus. News cameras were everywhere, magazine and newspaper cameramen were snapping photographs, and people were clamoring to have a picture made with her or an autograph signed. I was wholly embarrassed by the behavior of the homeless and volunteers alike, and I realized that I had utterly lost control of the situation and all semblance of a church service. Needless to say, there wasn't much time to visit, beyond a hello and good-bye, and I was sure I would never see her again—and I couldn't much blame her.

Several months passed, and as any Tuesday night will find me, I drove to The bridge for church. I parked my car in its usual place, and dreaded opening the door to get out. It was seven degrees in downtown Nashville, and this old Louisiana girl, who was raised in high heat and humidity, has still not adjusted to the cold weather of Tennessee after all these years. I slowly climbed out of the car, made my way to the microphone, opened in prayer, and let the praise music begin. My eyes scanned the audience, and my gaze fell on a bright yellow overcoat worn by a pretty lady with no make-up who was serving the homeless in the food line. I was quite taken aback because, much to my amazement, the "star" had returned. She had no fanfare, no body guard, no television news cameras to record her good deeds; she was there in simple anonymity. I thought to myself, "Do I ask her to sing, do I not ask her to sing? Will I insult her if I do, will I insult her if I don't? What is the right course of action?" This is not a dilemma that one is faced with every day—there's no manual for handling stars—so I decided I should ask.

I made my way to the other end of the bridge where she was serving macaroni from a large pot. "Is that you?" I awkwardly asked. "Yes, it's me," she answered smiling, and kept dipping from the pot. "Would you like to sing?" Another awkward moment. "No, I just came to serve, if that would be okay." I said of course it would be, and that we were glad to have her. "I brought my seven-year-old daughter tonight, too. She has been saving her allowance to give to you, to buy food for the homeless," she added.

I was floored. Here before me stands a woman who has graced the most prestigious stages and sung to adoring audiences around the world. She has performed for presidents and dignitaries, and has attained heights of success that most only dream of, yet she has chosen to assist homeless people under a bridge in the dead of winter on a cold Tuesday night. I was struck with the reality that she not only possessed the heart of a servant, but she has imparted the same rare qualities to her child, who is willing to give all of her possessions to care for the poor. At the end of the evening, mother and child strolled hand in hand to present her savings in a plastic sandwich bag. This seven-year-old child had saved enough one dollar bills, quarters, dimes, nickels, and pennies to buy 319 pounds of food to be served the next week on a cold Tuesday night under the bridge.

I will never forget that cold January night that I was allowed private insight into such a public figure. It was refreshing to see such a one who has kept herself unsoiled by the trappings of fame and success. I was happy to see that the young girl whom I had admired so much all those years ago was still very much the same. I admire her much more today than I did then.

God is love (1 John 4), and the love of the Father is shown through his children, be it pastor, churchgoer, layperson, gospel singer, music star, or her child.

Jesus built this church on love.

The Runaway

Recently my husband and I had lunch with a very successful real estate developer. We became acquainted at the urging of a mutual friend of ours who was also present at the meeting. In the early part of our conversation, I realized that John had visited the "church under the bridge" a few times, and had also brought his daughter, Arden.

During the course of our visit, John told us about a situation that he and Arden had encountered while with us under the bridge on the evening they had come with their church, Strong Tower. Their pastor, Chris, was bringing the message that evening, so Arden and John wanted to be there in support of him and The Bridge Ministry. Upon arriving, they were quickly put to work helping in the food line. Once the dinner service was over, they made their way to the outlying perimeter of the church service to hear the sermon and observe all that was going on around them.

As they stood there, Arden felt a tap on her shoulder and turned to see a very large man wanting to speak to her. She took a step behind her dad to hide herself from what she was unsure of. John turned to see what made Arden move behind him, and when he did, he saw the large man. This man's appearance was intimidating, to say the least. He was unshaven and dirty, wearing a dark shirt with the sleeves ripped out that displayed his massive, muscled arms. John had never met any of the Hell's Angels bikers, but imagined that this man would fit in well with them. John had arrived at the bridge still dressed from his work-day at the office, wearing a button-down shirt, khakis, and loafers, and instantly assessed that he was an easy target for being panhandled.

But what happened next would change all of their negative perceptions. "Can you help me?" the rough man asked. John replied, "Well, I'm not sure. What kind of help are you needing?" not yet wanting to commit himself until he knew his intentions. The gruff man then reached his hand out to a young boy standing close by and gently pulled him into our conversation. "You see this kid? He's a runaway. He's fifteen years old and his parents live in Kentucky. He ran away from home, and I've protected him for the last two days out here, and I need you to get him back to his parents before he gets hurt out on the streets."

John was stunned at this revelation. In a moment's time, John's opinion of this man changed dramatically—from Hell's Angel to angel of mercy. Here standing before John was a man with a gruff, hard exterior whom he would not have wanted to meet while walking through an alley, yet inside of him was the heart of a shepherd, caring for a little lost lamb.

An elder in John's congregation, who was with us under the bridge that night, is employed by the city. He has many connections and resources to handle these situations, so I recruited his help. Within a few hours this young runaway was returned safely home to his family, and his benefactor slipped into the darkness behind the bridge.

John and Arden were both greatly impacted by what they witnessed, and the opportunity that they were given to help. John never saw either of the two again, but he often thinks of how God brought two people from different worlds together to rescue a young boy. John hates to imagine what would have happened to that young man had this man not found him. But it warmed his heart to know that even on the streets, under a bridge, in the company of gang members and drug dealers, in the heart of what appeared to be a homeless brute, the love of God could still be found.

Chapter Six

Jesus on the Main Line

Prelude

"Which of you, if his son asks for bread, will give him a stone? Or
if he asks for a fish, will give him a snake? If you, then,
being evil, know how to give good gifts to your children,
how much more will your Father in heaven
give good gifts to those who ask Him!"

Matthew 7:9-11, NIV

Christmas time is my favorite time of the year. I enjoy giving gifts, so I start shopping early in the year to buy each person on my list that special present that I know will bring them joy. One particular Christmas when our son, Nicholas, was about four, I learned a valuable lesson about gift giving.

I had spent a great deal of time learning what all the popular toys for young boys were that year. I listened to the other mothers at K-4 outings to see what playthings their children desired, and I made sure to add those to my list. Nicholas was at a fun age and very excited about Christmas coming as he saw all the packages piling up under the tree for him. He would often go to the Christmas tree to shake his gifts and try to guess what was in each one. I could hardly wait for Christmas morning to arrive, to see the joy on his face when he opened them.

Early that Christmas morning he and Jasmine ran into our room just as dawn was breaking to wake us up. They were squealing with excitement as Kent and I dragged ourselves out of bed and made our way to the tree. All I could hear were the sounds of wrapping paper ripping, as it piled onto the floor of our family room. I watched as Nicholas tore into one gift right after the other, as if he were looking for something, not saying a word. After all of his gifts were opened, he said, "Where is my other gift?" I was taken aback. I said, "That is all of your gifts, son. There aren't any more." I thought to myself, "How could he want more? Have I raised him to be so spoiled that all of those toys didn't satisfy him?"

In perfect childlike innocence he tearfully said, "But, this wasn't what I wanted. This isn't what I asked for. Where is the toy I asked for?" Suddenly I realized that I had bought him the things I wanted him to have. It didn't matter that I had given him all the popular toys of the day; they weren't what Nicholas desired. I was so busy looking for what the other children would think was cool that I didn't stop to listen to his requests. So, we sat down and I asked him, "What is it that you want?" It wasn't that he was selfish or spoiled and wanting more;

Our son, Joshua Christmas, the night he preached under the bridge

what he actually wanted was one very small, inexpensive item. He had opened all the packages hoping to find it.

I have now learned to ask my children what they would like for Christmas. Every Christmas they make a detailed list all the things they want, and the colors and sizes they would like them in. I choose from their list, so that they are still surprised by good gifts, and I am not surprised by buying bad ones. I love giving, but especially to my children. Kent and I work very hard so that we can provide for them everything they need, but we also enjoy, on occasion, giving them what they *desire.* Jesus says that just as we enjoy giving in this way as a parent, our Heavenly Father, enjoys giving to us in this way also. He loves providing for our needs; but I also believe he enjoys giving us the desires of our heart. That is why we must tell him our specific needs and desires.

"Ask, and it will be given to you; seek, and you will find; knock, and it will be opened to you" (Matt. 7:7). This passage of Scripture tells us to ask and *it* will be given. What is *it*? *It* is the thing that you've told God you desire. Jesus is telling us that our Father won't give us a substitute, but he will give us the very thing that is asked of him. If you ask for one thing, he doesn't give you something in *its* place, He gives us what we've requested. If your child is hungry and asks for a fish, you wouldn't give him a snake, or for bread a rock. No, you give him what he hungers for.

Over the years I have learned to be more precise in my prayers. Instead of praying a blanket prayer of "Lord, *bless* my family today," I have learned to pray much more specifically. For example, when my husband got laid off from his job, I prayed: "Lord, my husband needs a better job with benefits." "Yet you do not have because you do not ask" (James 4:2). Jesus said that if we enjoy giving our children what they ask for, our Heavenly Father will give much more to you and me if we ask, so . . . *Tell Him What You Want!*

God Provides a Laptop

On several occasions I have encountered people passing the homeless and shouting at them to, "Get a job!" There is a common misconception about the homeless that they are dregs of society who have learned to "beat the system." Most people think the homeless just sit around the campfire all day, and draw a paycheck from the government for some feigned disability because they don't want to discipline themselves to work. I will be the first to admit that in the past I was among the many who held this opinion. I am not here to tell you that it doesn't happen, because I know that in some cases it does. However, I have found many of the homeless to hold jobs and be extremely hard workers. Many work day labor, bus tables, work construction, or mop floors and wash dishes in local restaurants. Did you know that it takes a full-time job of ten dollars an hour to afford a family dwelling? Many of the occupations that our friends are able to get work in are minimum wage jobs, all well below ten dollars an hour.

One evening I invited a local pastor whom I knew had a heart for the homeless to speak under the bridge. His brother had been an addict on the streets and had died there. During his sermon, he offered any of the homeless an eight dollar an hour job if they would just show up for work. Many of the people sitting in the congregation became excited and began quitting their minimum wage jobs to go to work for this pastor. Fifty-eight people showed up for work. While my pastor friend certainly meant well by this gesture, in the end it cost his congregation $55,000 in one month!

Over the years, God has brought folks into our ministry who want a better life for themselves and are willing to do what it takes to make that happen. Ricky is a young man whom I have come to love and respect. He is homeless and began attending our service about four years ago. He gave his heart to the Lord and became faithful to the church under the bridge. I quickly realized that he is a hard worker, that he desired a place to serve, and that he clearly has leadership qualities. I put him in charge of our small truck, where his responsibilities include organizing the loading and unloading of the chairs, lights, and sound system. This is a tedious job because there is a huge amount of equipment that has to fit into a small space. Everything must be well secured to insure that there is no damage done during transition from place to place. He also has been given a key to our warehouse where he volunteers every week. Ricky takes his work with us very seriously and does an excellent job.

Since we came to believe in him and trust him, he began to believe in himself. Ricky enrolled in a local college and is now in his second year of studies. Still homeless, he resides in a makeshift lean-to with no electricity, no running water, heat, or air conditioning. Yet, against all odds, he has made up his mind to better himself. His goal is to get a business degree and build a shelter for the homeless where they can also bring their pets.

Not long ago, one of the volunteers came to me during one of our church services. I could tell he was very disturbed. He asked me, "Are you aware that Ricky is falling behind in his studies?" I said that I was not aware. "He doesn't have a computer, and he's doing all of his research and studying manually. Does The Bridge Ministry have an extra laptop?" he asked. "No we don't. Let's pray and see what God will do. I know he desperately needs one." We began to pray. The next morning I had an early flight to Sacramento, California, to speak at a ladies conference. My heart was troubled for Ricky, and I prayed the entire flight for the miracle he so desperately needed.

I arrived in Sacramento and was greeted by a couple who are good friends and supporters of The Bridge Ministry. They had met me at the airport to take me to lunch and onto our final destination. In the course of our conversation, I mentioned Ricky's dilemma and how heavy my heart was for him. I began to tell them how proud we are of Ricky, and of all his accomplishments. I explained how he was now lagging behind in his studies and his need for a laptop in order to catch up. I noticed the couple responding strangely and exchanging knowing glances. I asked, "What is the matter?" They smiled at each other and then smiled at me and said, "We have a new laptop still in the box and never used. We have held onto it for a while and have never understood why, until now. We want to donate it to The Bridge Ministry for

Ricky working in the truck

Ricky." I was amazed! I could hardly believe my ears. Within a twenty-four hour time period, God answered our prayer! Ricky now has his laptop, and holds a 4.0 grade average.

I know that Jesus cares about Ricky and his dreams of a better life. Ricky could have given up on school, thrown his hands in the air, and said, "What's the use?" On the other hand, I could have gone in my own strength, maxed out my credit card to buy him a laptop, which in times past I would have done. However, we decided to wait on the Lord and see what he would do. "You have not, because you ask not."

Jesus on the Main Line, tell Him what you want . . . .

A Pair of Boots

I have seen God answer prayers and perform many miracles to sustain The Bridge Ministry in the last few years. However, it has been my desire to see the homeless "catch the faith" and see God work in their own lives personally. It goes along with the old saying, "Give the man a fish, feed him for a day. Teach him to fish, feed him for a lifetime." I have tried to teach the homeless to have faith in God for themselves.

There was a time I tried to be their all in all. In the early days of the ministry, I can remember driving all over town delivering everything from shoes to cold medicine, trying to meet every need. I realized that there is no end to the needs of the poor, that there is a "black hole" that can't be filled by me, only by God. I can remember thinking, "I would die for these people if it would help them." Then I realized, "There is no need for me to. Jesus already did."

While John was in prison, he sent his disciples to Jesus. They asked, "Are You the Coming One, or do we look for another?" Jesus answered and said to them, "Go and tell John the things you have seen and heard: that the blind see, the lame walk, . . . the poor have the gospel preached to them" (Luke 7:18-22). In essence what he told them was: "The blind man went away with what he needed—sight. The lame man went away with what he needed—to walk. The poor man went away with what he needed—money? No! The poor had the gospel preached to them." The takeaway message is that if we preach the gospel to the poor, the gospel will help them in every dire situation. That realization liberated me.

There is a young man on the streets of Nashville whom I love dearly. He is very gentle and soft spoken, a severe alcoholic, yet there is something intangible that sets him apart from others under the bridge. We'll call him David. I have known him and fed him for quite some time. He sits in church under the bridge and weeps in the presence of God. One night I asked him, "David, what is it about you? You are different from the others." "My dad is a pastor in Little Rock, and my sister is a missionary to Africa," he answered. "I have been through seminary, and I know the gospel." Homelessness is a lifestyle that David has chosen, and for the life of me, I can't understand why. He is educated, nice looking, and I think he has a lot to offer any community, and under the right circumstances, the body of Christ. My heart breaks for him. I long to see him set free. I fully believe that if God had sent me to the streets for one person, he sent me there for David. Because of the prayers of his dad in Little Rock, I know with all of my heart that I will see David saved and set free.

I had been teaching under the bridge on the subject: If God can feed the sparrow, and clothe the lily, he will feed and clothe you, if you will ask. Little did I know that David was walking the streets of Nashville in shoes that were torn to shreds. His toes were touching the pavement as he walked and his feet had begun to bleed. He was walking with his girlfriend to the stadium downtown, and mentioned to her the pain he felt in his feet. She turned to him and said, "Ms. Candy said to ask and you shall receive. Why don't you ask God for new shoes?" David turned his face to the open skies over Nashville and lifted his voice to God and said, "Lord! I need a pair of boots, size 10 ½." They continued on with their trek to the stadium. Later that night, they were walking back to where they were camped, and as they walked, a pair of brown work boots came into view, lying beside the road. As they looked closer, they realized they were holding a new pair of $150 work boots, size 10 ½!

This excited David, his girlfriend, and all of the other homeless, when I had him share his testimony under the bridge, of how Jesus heard his prayer. David is still homeless, and he is still an alcoholic. I believe that if God hears a homeless man's "boot prayers," he is still hearing a dad's prayers in Little Rock for a son named David who lives on the streets of Nashville. He's still Jesus on the Main Line, Tell Him What You Want!

A Scooter for Bo

When feeding people over a period of time, and watching them come to the knowledge of Jesus Christ, and seeing them grow in their walk with him, you cannot help but grow attached to them. Some of the dearest friends I have are people I have come to know and cherish from under the bridge.

One of these friends is "Bo." Bo first came to us merely for a hot meal, and like most of the homeless, was at first quite skeptical. He was always polite, but lingered toward the back of the bridge and for the most part kept to himself. Bo is quite overweight and has a very kind face, which made me think I'd like to know his story, so I sought him out. I learned that he had no addictions to drugs or alcohol and that somewhere in his past he had a wife and family. The pressures of life made him leave home one day and never return. Following the railway tracks and hopping trains, he came to rest in Nashville.

I began to see that he was very attentive in the church services, and on one summer Tuesday evening he came forward and gave his heart to the Lord Jesus. My husband and I soon made arrangements to take him to a local church that had a baptistery, and my husband baptized him in water.

Over time, Bo began to develop health conditions which made it very difficult to walk to the bridge on Tuesdays. I noticed that he would arrive at church later and later, and from time to time he wasn't able to come at all. I grew very concerned. Then I noticed that his legs had swollen to such a point that they were discolored and began to ooze.

One of our volunteers gave him a bed in their home and cared for him. His fever had risen and the towels they had placed on his legs would fill with fluid and had to be changed hourly. We were afraid that Bo would die.

After much prayer and medical attention, he began to recover. I knew that Bo would no longer be able to continue the trek through the city on foot to come to church. I had visited a local car lot in search of a box truck for the ministry, and while there noticed a beautiful red, motorized wheelchair, and Bo came to mind. "Wow! That's really pretty!" I exclaimed to the salesman, "How much does it cost?" He quickly informed me that it was being sold on consignment for a lady who had bought it for her ailing husband. The man had passed away before the scooter could be used, so it was brand new. The price of the scooter was $6,000. The lift that went with it would be another $3,000.

I boldly said, "I know a homeless man who needs that scooter! Would you ask the lady what her bottom dollar is?" "I sure will," he replied, "but what is your top dollar?" I didn't want tell him that at that moment I couldn't have given him $50. The ministry was strapped. I went home to pray.

I told the Lord how badly Bo needed that scooter. I earnestly prayed, quoted Bible verses to the Lord to remind him of his Word, and walked the floor. I prayed every morning and a week passed, "Lord, Bo needs that scooter." I prayed two weeks, then three. I still heard no word from the salesman. Luke 18 tells a story about a widow pleading her cause to an unjust judge. The judge finally grants her wish because she began to weary him. I love what Jesus says, "And shall God not avenge His own elect who cry out day and night to Him, though He bears long with them? I tell you that He will avenge them speedily" (Luke 18:1-8).

Sometimes God tarries long. There are prayers that I have prayed for years, that I continue to pray still, knowing that when he answers, he will answer speedily. Jesus finishes his thought with this question, "When he comes will he find faith?" I find that the enemy can render me powerless if he can rob me of my faith. I find that I, as a Christian, am in a constant struggle to hold tightly to the things I believe. It's not a struggle with temptation to fall, but a battle in my mind to walk by faith when the things I see contradict the promises of God.

Six weeks later, on a Tuesday afternoon, I was in our family room on my knees praying for the upcoming hours under the bridge. I heard Kent climb the stairs and enter the room, so I lifted my head to see what the matter was. Very calmly he said, "The car lot just called and said for you to come get your scooter. They had purchased it from the lady who owned it, and are donating it to us for Bo!"

Jesus on the Main Line, Tell Him What You Want....

Chapter Seven

Troubles of This World

Prelude

This poor man cried out, and the LORD heard him,
And saved him out of all his troubles.

Psalm 34:6

My husband Kent and I have been married for more than two decades. In the not-too-distant future, we will be celebrating our silver wedding anniversary. When first married, I never understood that so many years of marriage could be so fulfilling. I am pleased to find that the longer we are together the sweeter our relationship grows.

It is very nice growing older as a couple, because as I see indications of aging in myself, I also notice them in my husband. I'm not really excited about wrinkles, aches and pains, or forgetfulness, and I plan to fight it as long as I can, but it is comforting that as I age I am not alone in my struggle. For example, when I finally broke down and bought reading glasses, Kent was sympathetic because he needed them too. And in the evenings, if I have dozed while watching our favorite television show, I often find that Kent is asleep in the recliner next to me.

I once heard about an older couple who were watching television one evening. During the commercial break, the husband suddenly stood up. "I'm going to the kitchen for a bowl of ice cream," he announced. "Would you like for me to get you a bowl too?" "Yes, that would be wonderful, thank you," she replied. "But, I would like nuts on mine. Would you mind?" Her husband agreed, and off to the kitchen he went.

In a few minutes the wife could hear her husband in the kitchen clanging pots and pans, and she noticed he was taking an unusually long time. Much later he arrived back into the family room with two large plates. "What took you so long?" his wife asked. "Well, it just took a while to scramble our eggs," he said, handing her a plate. She looked at the eggs and said, "I thought I told you I wanted cheese on mine."

However wonderful growing older in a relationship can be, there are certain drawbacks that I have noticed. I have become so familiar with Kent and his likes and dislikes, his political, religious, and social views, that I often anticipate his thought in conversation. Occasionally, without thinking, I interrupt him to finish his sentences before he has the chance to complete his thought. I'm sure this is annoying to him, but he is very patient with me. I am trying hard to discipline myself to break this bad habit, because, in so doing, I realize that indeed I did not know what he was saying. Even though I have been married to him for a long time, I am still learning things about him that pleasantly surprise me. He has knowledge on a variety of subjects that I had not given him credit for knowing, and if I will stop to listen fully to what he is saying, I might learn something. There is an old southern expression that says, "I was broadcasting, when I should have been tuning in." Or in other words, I was talking when I should have been listening.

Believers may sometimes do this with God. We often become so familiar with his Word that we take bits and pieces of what his Word says and don't allow him to complete his sentence. If we "tuned in" a little better, we might find that we would be pleasantly surprised. I once heard someone say, "You know the Bible says, 'Many are the afflictions of the righteous,' and I've found that verse to be so true." Sadly, the remainder of the verse went unspoken. Yes, "Many are the afflictions of the righteous," but God doesn't leave us hanging there. If you allow him to finish the sentence, he says, *"But the Lord delivers him out of them all"* (Ps. 34:19).

Michael Lash was a homeless man who had been a member of the church under the bridge for quite some time. Over the years, we have become good friends. Early on, as I would see him, he would attend church quite inebriated and broken. I remember him as polite and very intelligent, and I knew that he possessed the potential to do much greater things. He had addictions to overcome, due to many adversities early in his life. He had been raised by his mother whom he

(L-R) Candy Christmas, Michael Lash, Kent Christmas

loved dearly, but she passed away when Michael was eleven years old. He was raised in foster care until his adoption, but later was sent back to foster care.

He spent the early part of his life in and out of trouble, never feeling that he belonged; so he found his home on the streets of Nashville. Alcoholism became a way of life, but without funds for liquor, he resorted to drinking mouthwash and rubbing alcohol to feed his demons. Highly intoxicated, Michael awoke in the middle of the night in a pool of blood, with the blood vessels in his throat bursting and his life pouring out onto the campsite ground. He knew that he was dying, and began to pray to God for a second chance. Psalm 34:6 says, "This poor man cried out, and the Lord heard him . . . ." That night there was a deliverance in Michael's life. In his brush with death, he made a decision to call on the Lord. He has been alcohol free and sober for two years. Michael realized that he could not defeat his enemy of alcoholism on his own, so he put his trust completely upon the Lord. Without interruption, God was able to complete his work in Michael's life, and thus finish the Scripture verse: "And saved him out of all his troubles."

Financial Turmoil

In early 2009, we watched helplessly as America's financial system began to reveal flaws and seemed to unravel before our eyes. The stock market was on a steady decline as daily news media outlets began to report bank closings at a record rate. Large companies that previously seemed impervious to economic recession began filing for bankruptcy protection. Joblessness was escalating. Reversals in our financial markets even resulted in a downturn in the housing markets, slowing buying and construction to a snail's pace. The automotive industry also suffered as dealerships closed their doors, and unemployment lines grew.

This was an unsettling time for much of America, as well as for many churches and nonprofit organizations. The Bridge Ministry was no exception. Our financial support had always come through private contributions and aid from local businesses, many of which were construction-related companies. Our top four donors had terminated their giving because of their own bankruptcy filings or the need to save their families from financial disaster. Almost overnight, contributions dropped fifty percent. What was once a shoestring budget was now becoming almost no budget at all. Our financial hardship was compounded by the fact that the number of the poor we served was also growing. We found ourselves caring for many more families with children who had been forced to move to shelters or live in their automobiles due to losing homes to foreclosure.

I vividly remember one particular occasion during this time when we were serving dinner and the serving line seemed endless. About four hundred people had formed two lines along the bridge waiting to be served. As usual, I was walking through the lines greeting those who had come, shaking hands, making conversation. I stepped up to a middle-aged woman and smiled and extended my hand to shake hers. She stared at me for a moment and said, "Are you Candy Christmas?" I smiled and nodded that I was. "Oh, no!" she exclaimed. "I've watched you sing on television and I have always wanted to meet you, but not like this!" she began to sob. "My husband has lost his job and we lost our home. We are homeless, and I am so ashamed to meet you this way." I put my arm around her reassuringly as she cried, and I found it hard to find words to say.

Many nights during this time, I found myself awake in the wee hours of the morning feeling that I carried the weight of the world. I walked the floors talking to the Lord, telling him all about my troubles, and the troubles of the friends I had come to love so dearly. I acutely felt the pain of the poor and I constantly reminded God of his Word and his promises concerning them. I had always looked to our donors as our source for help, and now, due to no fault of their own, they could no longer help me carry the financial load at this critical time. I had only one source to place my hope. I believe that God wanted me to change my focus from earthly resources, and trust only him as our Source.

I remembered the biblical passage: "Then the LORD said to Moses, 'Behold, I will rain bread from heaven for you. And the people shall go out and gather a certain quota every day, that I may test them, whether they will walk in My law or not. And it shall be on the sixth day that they shall prepare what they bring in, and it shall be twice as much as they gather daily'" (Exod. 16:4-5). The Israelites were given manna from heaven. They were only given provision enough for their needs that day, except for the Sabbath. They were allowed to gather and store extra only for the day of rest.

This principle of trusting God was carried into the New Testament when Jesus' disciples came to him and said, "Lord, teach us to pray" (Luke 11:1). Jesus begins to pray and he includes this request, "Give us this day our daily bread" (Matt. 6:11). He never taught them to pray for a storehouse to store for the future. He was tutoring them in being completely dependent upon the Heavenly Father to supply their daily needs. This walk of faith is not an easy one, but I believe that sometimes God allows these lean times to come our way to show us that he can be trusted to supply "our daily bread."

Did you know that the Bible is made of sixty-six books, thirty-nine in the Old Testament (929 chapters) and twenty-seven books in the New Testament (260 chapters), and 23,214 verses? The center of the

Bible is Psalm 118. There are 594 chapters before and 594 chapters that follow. If you add all the chapters in the Bible except Psalm 118, they total 1188. The center verse of the Bible is Psalm 118:8, "It is better to trust in the Lord than to put confidence in man." I guess you might say that this is the "central theme" of the Bible.

We survived this very difficult time by trusting in the Lord. I emerged with a stronger faith and a greater assurance of the faithfulness of God. I can't exactly tell you how we managed, because it doesn't work out on paper. There was no parting of the sea, no manna that fell, but we received our daily bread as Peter wrote in 2 Peter 1:1, 4, "to those who have obtained like precious faith . . . by which have been given to us exceedingly great and precious promises, that through these you may be partakers of the divine nature," to overcome . . . *The Troubles of This World.*

The Box Truck Story

My motto has always been "Give the homeless so many things that they will need help in carrying it away." So I realized that I needed a large box truck. We would need to transport goods and supplies to the outreaches every week, as well as travel throughout the city to receive donations from local establishments. The Lord had given Kent and me a good Christian friend, Bob, who is a car dealer in the Nashville area. Bob is a big-hearted man and has a desire to help the poor. I called him one day and mentioned that I needed a big box truck with a lift on the back, and I asked him to let me know if he found a good deal on one.

Unknown to me, Bob was then on a mission. He searched car auctions and used car lots for weeks, and made inquiries of his many friends, until he found "just the right truck for me." He found a truck with a newly built engine; he then had the box removed and a new twenty-six-foot box mounted. He then removed the lift gate from the back and found a newer and better model, and had it attached to the new box. My friend Bob had gone well beyond the call of duty or friendship, truly making a tremendous sacrifice for the work of the Lord.

When all of this work on the truck was completed, he called Kent and me to come get it. When we walked around it, we wept. It was so beautiful and so needed—much more truck than we could have hoped for. Bob sold it to us for a fraction of its worth, even less than what he himself had in it. We were elated, to say the least.

Soon after purchasing the truck, we were busy sending it all over the city to pick up load after load, filling up our warehouse with food. On a hot, humid June day we went to the local food bank and filled our new truck with perishable items. The temperature was approaching the one hundred degree mark. On this particular day, I wasn't able to find another driver, so I asked my husband to drive for me. We had a visiting minister in town from New York City who went with us, and he was dressed in a suit and tie. I was traveling back to the warehouse in my car, quite a distance ahead of Kent and the pastor in the box truck. My cell phone rang and it was Kent. "I'm not sure why, but the truck has stopped, and I am on the side of the road. Could you turn around and come back?" I was about twenty minutes from them by this time, but I turned the car around to find them. By the time I made it to where they were parked on the side of the road, Kent had the hood of the truck raised. He was perspiring profusely, covered in grease, and looking very grim. I looked in the cab of the truck and there sat our dear visitor from New York, still in suit and tie, with sweat rolling down his face. No bright smiles to be found.

My brothers own a bus company and have mechanics in their employ. They repair diesel engines, so if all else fails, I call my brothers. Right? I called a tow truck, which appeared two hours later and towed our truck to my brothers' establishment. The tow truck driver parked our truck in such a way that the back door was blocked and the spoiling food could not be unloaded. The rising stench of rotting food only compounded my stress.

The next day my brother, Trent, called and asked, "Are you sitting down?" I wasn't, but I told him I was. "My mechanics have looked at the engine of your truck and it will cost $21,000 to repair it. It looks as if a grenade was detonated in the engine, and it must be replaced." My ears were ringing, and I felt myself unable to breath, knowing that the cost of the repair was much more than we had paid for the truck itself! I thanked him and hung up the phone.

In the Bible the book of Isaiah says, "No weapon formed against you shall prosper" (54:17). It says, it "shall not prosper"; it didn't say, "It shall not be formed." In the past, my faith response would have been simply to crumble at the sight of the weapon being formed. But not this time.

I instantly went to my knees in prayer. I put The Bridge Ministry and all of our work with the poor on the altar of my heart. I said, "Lord, The Bridge Ministry isn't mine, it belongs to you. If you are wanting to shut us down, it belongs to you, and I won't stand in your way. Shut it down. If you want us to continue, then the truck is yours, and it's your problem. I need you to fix your truck." I understand that nothing I have belongs to me. It all belongs to him. It's his responsibility to "supply my needs according to his riches in glory." "Casting all your care upon Him, for He cares for you" (1 Pet. 5:7).

Soon the phone rang and it was my friend Bob Farr, as always, wanting to help. He had found a truck engine that had been rebuilt with a one-year warranty, for $5,000 dollars, and wanted to know if we wanted it. We said, "Yes," and he offered to pay half. My brothers called a few moments later and said, "We've talked it over, and our company would like to donate the labor to install your engine." In a few minutes time, we had gone from owing $21,000 to $2,500. All we needed to pay for was half an engine, which would be installed free.

I have always been the kind of person who never liked telling my troubles. Call it pride, call it whatever you want, but usually if there is a need in my life you will never know it. If you ask me how I'm doing, I'll say "Blessed." I've decided that God is God and he doesn't need my help. Me telling my troubles to everyone around me isn't faith, it's whining. If I whined and complained to get people to meet my needs, then it was me and people, not God who made the way.

Kent and I had decided that we wouldn't announce the situation about the truck. We still owed $2,500 that we didn't have, so God would need to complete the miracle. In the course of the next week, people came into my office who had never donated to The Bridge Ministry before. One man came in with a check for $1,500, another with $500, then $250, and a couple of checks for $100.

"Give, and it will be given to you: good measure, pressed down, shaken together, and running over will be put into your bosom" (Luke 6:38). Only my Father is able to make triumphs from . . . *The Troubles of This World.*

Beauty from Ashes

I would like to write this book and lead you to believe that every dealing I have had with my friends on the street has been joyous. I'd love nothing more than to make you feel warm and fuzzy about working with the homeless, so that you would be motivated to get involved. I would like to tell you that I have never been lied to, scammed, stolen from, cursed at, or taken advantage of; but the truth of the matter is, I have. The path that I have chosen is not for the faint of heart, and I have made up in my mind not to get discouraged or disheartened. Jesus said, "Blessed is he who is not offended because of me" (Matt. 11:6).

There is an element among the homeless who are con artists, felons, thieves, and panhandlers, and it takes a while for someone who works

Worshiping under the bridge

regularly with them to become what I like to call "street smart." In the early days of the ministry, we gave away many pairs of new shoes still in the box and new clothing with the tags still attached. I came to find out that on most Wednesday mornings after the Tuesday night service under the bridge, there was a huge garage sale downtown in front of the city library—selling the articles we had given away the night before. We have since learned to remove all tags from clothing and to exchange new shoes for the old ones because it is very difficult for them to resell shoes that have already been worn. No matter how badly the new articles of clothing are needed, many times there is an addiction screaming inside them demanding that they sacrifice their own needs for another "fix."

I wish I knew how much money I have given to people to purchase bus tickets to go home to visit their "dying mothers" or to buy some badly needed prescription medication that actually went to buy meth or crack cocaine. I regret my ignorance, but I now have a PhD in "street smarts"!

On many occasions I encountered a young man who told me that he had AIDS. I prayed with him often, we fed him and gave him rides to the doctor; and as he presented prescriptions for his disease, I often gave him money to fill them. He had such a special place in our hearts and all of the volunteers took special attention and great care of J. R. as we watched him waste away to skin and bones before our eyes. My heart broke for him, as I watched him die.

Before long J. R. no longer came to the bridge and for at least a year we all assumed the worst. One night, a nice white car drove up and parked beside the bridge as we were singing. Out of the car emerged a huge, overweight J. R. I could not believe my eyes. He strolled over to me, accompanied by a very nice looking, mild mannered lady, and introduced her to me as his wife. He had come to the bridge that night to apologize to me. He told me that month after month he had lied to me about his having AIDS, that the prescriptions that he had presented to me were falsified, and that he had bilked me out of hundreds of dollars. He told me that the Hound from Heaven (the Holy Spirit) followed him everywhere he went, that he had trouble sleeping and was completely miserable until he repented and gave his heart to Jesus. He said that, in fact, it was my innocent trust in him, that he had misused, which was the very thing that God used to lead him to Christ.

J. R. is now a thriving Christian, a homeowner, and family man. He is employed at a local church as maintenance man and custodian. He is an asset to the community and to the body of Christ.

The Apostle Paul reminds us in the book of Romans that "all things work together for good to those who love God, to those who are the called according to His purpose" (8:28). Even in my ignorance, God turned for his glory ... *the Troubles of This World.*

Chapter Eight

Precious Lord

Prelude

*"Whereby are given unto us exceeding great
and precious promises: that by these ye might be
partakers of the divine nature. . . ."*

2 Peter 1:4, KJV

As a young Christian I admit that I struggled to read the Bible. It was hard for me to get past the "thees" and "thous" and the "begets," but I forced myself to read a certain number of chapters a day. I found reading Scripture to be like eating green vegetables—I didn't like it, but I knew it was good for me. It was hard to discipline myself to sit and read during the day, so usually I would try to read the Bible at bedtime. Reading my Bible became a wonderful sleep aide; I was out like a light almost the moment I opened the book. I found myself reading

the same verse over and over trying to keep my eyes open, and consequently, I wasn't retaining much of what I read. Before long I was by-
passing my Bible reading and going on to sleep.

I felt like the little boy whose mother wanted him to pray at night
before he went to bed. She bought a plaque and hung it on the wall
over his bed. Every night before he went to sleep, he knelt by his bed,
folded his hands, looked up at the plaque, and read, "Now I lay me
down to sleep. I pray the Lord my soul to keep . . . ." He soon grew bored
of this ritual, so he began to crawl under the covers, lie in bed, look up
at the plaque, and read, "Now I lay me down to sleep, I pray the Lord
my soul to keep. . . ." He soon grew tired of this also. Then one night he
crawled in bed, looked up at the plaque, and said, "There it is Lord, you
can read it for yourself."

It was later in my walk with God that I found his promises "precious." The word "precious" means rare, of great price, especially dear,
or valued greatly. In times of trials and hopelessness, I needed reassur-
ance from God's Word that everything would turn out for my good.
His Word became precious. That which once was mundane reading,
became my lifeline and especially dear.

The word "precious" is used seven times in the writings of 1 and 2
Peter. Peter speaks of God's promises as precious, but also our faith as
"precious." "*Simon Peter, a servant and an apostle of Jesus Christ, to
them that have obtained like precious faith*" (2 Pet. 1:1, KJV). If you
own a "precious gemstone" that is valuable, it is because there aren't
many of its kind to be found. It is rare. It is the same with faith. God

tries our faith, to make it more valuable and especially dear to him, because it is a rare faith that will trust him through the trial. Precious promises given to those of precious faith.

"But with the precious blood of Christ, without blemish and without spot" (1 Pet. 1:19). We lived in Louisiana when I was a child, and at one time there was a shortage of blood in our state. An urgent announcement came over the radio waves over and over. A resident of New Orleans had a disease and needed a blood transfusion, but the AB negative blood type was very rare. They were asking anyone who had this rare blood type to please donate blood to save this person's life. This blood was *precious,* or valuable and hard to find.

There was a disease loosed on planet earth through Adam called sin. Only one blood type could save the human race. It was blood of great price, rare and greatly valued. Only blood without sin or spot could take away the sins of the world—only the *precious* blood of Jesus Christ!

We had a dear family friend, Pastor James McFall, who has now gone on to be with the Lord. A few years ago, he called our home and began telling me about a class for young ministers he had started in his church. He told me about a young man he was now mentoring, who was the son of a pastor from a nearby town. This young man had been raised in church, but his life had gotten off course and he had become hooked on drugs. Pastor McFall said that this young man had gotten so low in his life that he had decided to commit suicide. He loaded his 357 magnum pistol and drove his truck to an obscure place down a country road. He placed the nose of the pistol to his temple and pulled the trigger. There was a click, but the pistol didn't fire. He pointed the gun out the open window and pulled the trigger, and this time it fired loudly, the gunshot ringing through the woods. He assumed that the pistol had been jammed and that now the problem was fixed.

Once again he placed the pistol's barrel to his temple, squinting his eyes in anticipation of the gun's blast. The trigger clicked, but again it wouldn't fire. Then fear gripped the heart of this young pastor's son who had desperately tried to take his own life. He became acutely aware that he had witnessed supernatural intervention. He began to weep, there alone in his pickup truck, with his weapon lying in his lap. He felt the Spirit of God wrapping his arms around him, and he heard him say, "Son, if you're finished with your life, give it to me. I'll take it." He gave his heart to Jesus, and has accepted the call to preach the gospel. For many years he sat under the ministry and tutelage of Pastor McFall, making great strides in faith and maturity.

I too was raised in the home of a pastor. Our lives were always filled with church functions, Bible studies, Easter Cantatas, Christmas pageants, children's church, ladies meetings, and the list goes on and on. I can speak for myself in saying that it is easy to get bored with church and to take sacred things for granted. The Holy Spirit is a gentleman and will never force himself upon us, so he patiently waited for me to realize my need for him. When religion became ritualism, and I became disinterested from the monotony of church going, I searched for other things to fill the void in my life. When I could not find peace or joy in life, I called out to him. It was then that the humdrum and ordinary became precious. It was then that my faith became much more than ceremonial; it became a true relationship with Jesus Christ.

I love the words of the song, *Precious Lord,* which are just as powerful today as they were in 1932 when they were penned by Thomas A. Dorsey. He was a young husband and father grieving the loss of his wife and new-born infant, whose life spanned only a few short moments. Thomas Dorsey wrote: "Through the storms through the night, lead me on to the Light." In his anguish, he verbalized his cry for help to Christ Jesus, whom he had found so precious during this time. Whether it's the loss of a loved one, the burdens of ministry, the blindness of sin, or the painful darkness of addictions, he will hear your cry. He gave us precious promises to strengthen our precious faith, because he is our . . . *Precious Lord.*

Lyrics That Heal

It is fascinating that the landmark experiences in my walk with the Lord were not while standing on a stage singing, or even while serving the poor under the bridge, but they are times in the wee hours of the morning I've spent alone with him. Times when everything is quiet and dark, and the rest of the family is sleeping, before the hustle and bustle of the morning begins, when I have found a secret place under the shadow of the Almighty. It's in these times that I have felt him so close, and have poured my heart out to my dearest Friend, without interruption. I find that early in the morning my mind is not yet clouded with the cares of life, and I can focus solely on my fellowship with Christ.

One morning in particular, my eyes opened early, and I was instantly awakened before the alarm was set to sound. I quietly climbed out of bed, as not to disturb my husband, and I found my way to the coffee pot, then to my familiar place of prayer, an old chair that my grandmother had given me before she passed away.

I began to sip my coffee in the darkness and talk to Jesus. I had many pressures weighing heavily on me concerning the ministry, and I was seeking answers as well as a refuge. There was friction in the office among some of my workers, and as always, I was trying to run a ministry on a shoestring budget. All of these things together made me weary.

As I knelt there, an old song came to my mind, one that I had not heard in many years. I couldn't remember the words correctly, but I began to sing it to an audience of One. I pictured the face of Jesus, and I sang it to him:

Precious Lord, take my hand
Lead me on, let me stand
I am tired, I am weak, I am worn
Through the storm, through the night
Lead me on to the light
Take my hand precious Lord, lead me home

As I sang that song softly in the darkness, the Spirit of the Lord flooded my heart as the tears began to flow. When I had come to Jesus that morning I was burdened and heavy. I now felt light and refreshed. I continued to sing it over and over, and didn't want to stop. The daylight came, and soon began the rush of preparing for a Tuesday at the office, and getting my children dressed and off to school. I forgot about my morning devotion, and went on with my daily routine.

It was a cool autumn evening and pleasant weather for street ministry. A large crowd showed up for church under the bridge, and I had taken the microphone to welcome everyone. As I spoke, the song "Precious Lord" resurfaced in my mind, along with the thoughts of how it had ministered to me that very morning. I turned to the piano player and asked, "Do you know the song 'Precious Lord'?" He nodded as if to say he did, and he began to play it softly, and I began to lead the congregation. Once again, as we sang, the sweetness of the Holy Spirit began to sweep gently across the congregation. I could see heavy hearts, worn and weary faces being transformed before my eyes. Tears flowed and trickled down their weary faces as they sang, "I'm so tired, I am weak, I am worn." That night lives were changed and many lost souls were saved.

Three weeks later on a Tuesday night, a very tall striking African-American young man stepped up to speak with me. He had a wide, open grin and asked, "Do you remember me?" I had a faint recognition of him, but couldn't place from where. "Where do I know you from?" I replied smiling. "Do you remember the other night when you sang 'Precious Lord take my hand'?" "Yes, of course I do," I answered. "I was here that night in the church service, and I gave my heart to Jesus that night. My life was changed completely," he added. "That old song you sang made

"Precious Lord, take my hand..."

me think of my mother, whom I had not seen in years. I've been a drug addict living on the streets, and didn't want her to see the state I was in."

"After that night, I traveled back home to see her and I've come back to Nashville to enter drug rehab. I will be there 120 days. I came here to ask you if you would pray for me while I'm there, that God would complete the miracle in my life." I hugged him and promised that I would pray.

Dancing for Joy under the Bridge

Many times throughout the years I have asked the homeless for a show of hands of how many of them were raised in church. Invariably, ninety percent or more will raise their hands indicating that they were raised in the home of churchgoers, went to Sunday school, and were taught Bible verses. Many of the homeless know every stanza of the old hymns.

I have tried to make it our practice over the years that, in every church gathering under the bridge, we include one of the standard songs that the homeless might remember. The most requested song under the bridge, as you might imagine is, "Amazing Grace . . . that saved a wretch like me." I have noticed that something very special occurs when our congregation sings a hymn. It seems to impact their hearts like nothing else. I believe that is due to two things: the power of the hymn's message, and because it touches the roots of many of the homeless. I sense that for a moment these songs take them back home, to a more innocent time in their lives where they first came to the knowledge of Christ. It is my hope that this memory will rekindle a desire for a Christian lifestyle.

Every week our volunteers set up a sound system, musical instruments, chairs, and lights, and in a few short minutes a parking lot under a bridge is transformed into a sanctuary. We have a praise team that includes some of the most talented singers in Nashville; they skillfully sing the cutting edge praise choruses of the present day.

I know that this may seem odd to say, but if you can comprehend it, there is much joy in our worship on the streets. These are people who live in a constant state of despair and hopelessness, but when the music begins, they leave their troubles behind and rejoice in the Lord.

There is one sweet older gentleman who usually comes to church wearing no shoes. His feet are usually covered with dust, but without fail, he dances. As long as there is music, he flails his arms and dances with all of his might. Affectionately he's known as "the dancer." I have had new volunteers who've joined our security team come to me and ask, "Do you want me to stop him?" Think about it for a moment: here is a homeless man who lives outdoors in a makeshift dwelling, who lives in sadness, is searching for his next meal, has no shoes, and he's praising God. "No, don't stop him, let him dance," for Scripture says that "if they keep quiet, the stones will cry out" (Luke 19:40, NIV).

Another of the members of our "church under the bridge" is schizo-phrenic. He lives in a continual state of paranoia. This poor man believes the government and the president are all in a conspiracy against him, and he will talk as long as one can listen on this subject. When he walks away, you are left scratching your head thinking, "What did he just say?" Nevertheless, he has the voice of an angel. I gave him the name "Pavarotti" because, on many occasions, even before I came to know his real name, I've handed him a microphone and he began to sing "Precious Lord" and brought the house down. He has one of the most powerful voices I have ever heard. In reality, he may walk the streets of Nashville confused, but when we sing the hymns, his mind becomes clear and he sings under the power of God.

Not long ago I had the pleasure of having a well-known Christian comedian come to the bridge. I've seen this man captivate thousands of people and wow audiences around the world. When he drove up under the bridge he was visibly shaken, and I was surprised. "What's the matter," I asked? "I can't think of one thing that would be funny to a homeless person," he answered. "They are people," I replied. "They will laugh at the same things most people find funny."

Half-way through the praise and worship service, after noticing "the dancer" dancing and all the homeless people praising God, this young man came to me and was so excited. He said, "I get it. It's about joy. You are bringing them joy."

In the book of 1 Samuel, we read about King Saul being tormented by evil spirits. His servants invited David to play his harp for Saul to calm him. When David began to sing, the presence of God made the evil spirits depart, and the music soothed the soul of Saul (1 Samuel 16:14-23). To some degree I believe that this is the case for my friends under the bridge. They arrive depressed and anguished, but it is "joy unspeakable" when we sing praises unto the Lord. The dark cloud of their torment is lifted, sometimes forever, sometimes for a moment or an evening, but the relief cannot be contained.

Almost always it is the old hymn that strikes the heart chords . . . . *Precious Lord, Take My Hand.*

The Meth Addict

I'm not quite sure how or when I began this practice, but when the weather is nice and we're not rushed for time, I allow the homeless to take the microphone and sing. Usually I'll find one old hymn that everyone will recognize, and give three or four people a chance to sing the chorus through once. I try to keep control of it as best I can, a lesson I've learned the hard way.

I find that a few of our homeless people came to Music City with aspirations of becoming a musical sensation. Now, with dashed hopes, they still like to sing. Many are just normal people who never sang, but want a chance to stand and praise God. Occasionally, I'll pull people from this audience who leave me speechless by singing better than most professionals. This is very much a highlight in the service that the homeless look forward to. They love to cheer for one another, or point out shy ones to get them to sing, and we have great fun. I always say to them, "If you aren't brave enough to stand here and sing, you can't criticize those who do." That's the rule.

I like to pick a good mixture of singers, male, female, African American, and white. One night I was looking for a white female to croon a chorus of "Precious Lord." There was a woman whose face I was familiar with, and when she smiled I took her by the hand and lifted her from her chair.

As she stood, she whispered to me, "I don't really have a singing voice, but could I say something quickly?" I start getting a little nervous when the homeless try to deviate from the plan and, more times than not, I won't give them cart blanc with a microphone—I learned the hard way there too. Immediately, I felt a prompting of the Holy Spirit to let her speak.

She took the microphone into her shaking hand and said, "Y'all know me. I'm homeless and this is my church, the church under the

Candy Christmas with a friend under the bridge

bridge. I got saved here seven months ago, and I was a meth addict. When I got saved, I thought that would take the desire of drugs away from me. After I got saved, these people gave me a Bible that I began to read. The next day, the desire for drugs came over me, so strong, but I had received Jesus and didn't want to mess up. I took my Bible and began to read it. As I read it, I realized that the cravings for meth got weaker and went away. I learned to do that every day, until I crave it less and less. Jesus and his Word has helped me to be free and I have learned to depend on him. I have been drug free for seven months. Praise God!" *Precious Lord Take My Hand* . . . .

Chapter Nine

Could I Wish

Prelude

"Could I wish for me a palace here on earth below
While others called to missions suffer more than glad to go
Could I wish for fame and fortune wide acclaim to call my own
While others far more worthy bear the cross unknown."

When I was eleven, my parents moved me and my brothers from Louisiana to Nashville, to pursue gospel music. Nashville is known around the world as "Music City USA" and the home of country music and the legendary Grand Ole Opry. Since childhood I have had the pleasure of meeting and getting to know many of the country music legends, most of whom are Christians and lead very simple lives. It is humbling to meet those who are household names, and I feel blessed to have made their acquaintance.

If you drive through many of Nashville's neighborhoods, you will see the homes of the country music stars and industry moguls, and quickly see how success is measured here. Elaborate mansions, rolling estates, and fabulous automobiles are all "standards" of success. It is often said, "The guy who has the most toys at the end of his lifetime wins." It seems as if that is the typical mindset among many in the music industry.

Living in Music City, it's easy to get caught up in the rat race of desiring bigger and better, of wanting more and more—which soon becomes never enough. Before you realize it you are buying things that you don't need with money you don't have to impress people you don't like. But for the grace of God, I would still be on the treadmill of ever running and never arriving. I liken my experience to the Detroit auto manufacturers. I am told that every year when they need to upgrade their assembly lines to produce the new make and model for the upcoming year, they never add a little here and a little there for gradual change, but the factory is closed and all the employees are sent home for a short period of time. The machines are retooled to fit the new design and when the process is completed, then it's reopened for business.

For God to use me in all the ways I had asked him to, I needed to be retooled. My mindset needed adjustment and my convictions had to be changed. My assembly line had to be upgraded from the value system set by this world, so that I could see and desire greater riches of the kingdom of God. In his infinite mercy, he stopped my "production line," closed my doors, and sent me home for a season. I am so glad that the Master Builder knows all things and is still in control. This is a work that one cannot perform on oneself, but it's a work of grace, to make us vessels of honor for the Master's use. John the Baptist said, "I must decrease, and He must increase." I believe that it should be the desire of every Christian that, when others see us, we have decreased and Christ has increased to such a place that we are no longer seen, but only Christ in us. This is the measure of true success.

It takes the eyes of "Christ in us" to see what is truly valuable to God. Jesus makes the statement in Luke, "that which is highly esteemed among men is abomination in the sight of God" (Luke 16:15b, KJV). Later the Bible says, "Do not love the world or the things in the world. If anyone loves the world, the love of the Father is not in him" (1 John 2:15). In hindsight, I now see that I esteemed and even craved the things of this world. To be all that God had called me to be, I needed to possess the love of the Father.

One day we will stand before the throne of God where we will be in eager anticipation of receiving the reward for our service to him on this earth. I imagine that it is very possible that, as we stand before God in the company of those whom we have lauded as great and who seem so worthy, God will motion for us to stand aside, and then he will say, "Please make way for those in the back." Then trembling, some will step forward in their rags, the unknowns, the poor ministers whose bellies on this earth were never completely filled, who never owned an automobile or lived in a fancy dwelling, but who sacrificed all for the sake of the gospel. These are spoken of in Hebrews, "And others had trial of cruel mockings and scourgings, yea, moreover of bonds and imprisonment: They were stoned, they were sawn asunder, were tempted, were slain with the sword: they wandered about in sheepskins and goatskins; being destitute, afflicted, tormented; (Of whom the world was not worthy)" (Heb. 11:36-38, KJV).

Do I believe that we must become poor and unknown to carry the gospel of Christ? No, I don't. But we must always keep in mind that a servant is never above his Master (Matt. 10:24). We serve a King who came to this world through a stable. He "was manifested in the flesh" (1 Tim. 3:16), who lived on this earth homeless, and had no place to lay his head (Matt. 8:20). He was Creator of all things (John 1:3), yet he lived the life of a humble carpenter. Jesus has never asked of us anything that he himself has not already done. The book of Hebrews tells us, "looking unto Jesus, the author and finisher of our faith, who for the *joy* that was set before Him endured the cross" (12:2). After seeing this, then we read with clarity his words,"If anyone desires to come after Me, let him deny himself, and take up his cross" (Matt. 16:24). This self sacrifice is the way of Christ. As Paul wrote, he considers all things rubbish (Phil. 3:8, NIV).

The church in America has set the "bar" so high that struggling missionaries or pastors of small congregations, whose lives of ministry are spent in obscurity and anonymity, whose faces never grace the television screen, nor sport the lasted fashion, who have written no books, or have no degree to their credit, are looked down on and branded as failures. Only those who can see through the "eyes of Christ" can see that there are "giants in God" in paupers clothing who walk humbly among us. I'd like to be counted in their number. It would be an honor that when the "roll is called up yonder," my name is mentioned in the company of theirs. That, for me, would be the height of success. The words of a song are ringing in my ears, "If I'm the soldier of an army, whose captain hung on a tree, then *could I wish* some easy life for me."

Going to Haiti

My husband and I live in a modest, older home north of Nashville in the small community of Goodlettsville. We purchased our home when our children were small, thinking that later we would find a newer one, with bigger rooms, and possibly more acreage. We never intended to stay here as long as we have. There are many things about our house that frustrate me. For example, the electrical wiring is outdated and you can't run the microwave oven while the toaster is in use because you'll trip a breaker and the whole house goes dark. The plumbing is antique, so the pipes are leaky, and the garbage disposal seems to always back up when we have company on the way over.

About the time my husband and I decided that it would be nice to "fix-up" our dinosaur for resale, the housing market took a hit, and houses virtually stopped selling. Furthermore, most of our savings had been spent to feed the homeless and give to the poor, so it seemed that our answer was clear. We would keep our sweet old dinosaur that was full of our family memories, give it a little tender love and care, and stay put.

Jasmine with Haitian orphans showing off their new sunglasses!

In 2009, I was invited by a friend to take a mission trip to Haiti. Her dad is a missionary there, and we had been sending food and supplies from our warehouse to this ministry. My son, Nicholas, and I quickly accepted the invitation, as I was eager to see the missionary work there, but also wanted my son to be impacted by the reality of how most of the world lives.

We planned and packed, and the day finally came when we arrived in Port au Prince, Haiti. As we flew low across the city to make our landing into the airport, Nicholas and I noticed that there were mostly shanties and huts, instead of buildings and skyscrapers lining the sky. As we stepped off the plane, we were struck with the humidity and the salty taste of the tropical air. Everyone was wet with perspiration, and the smell of sweat filled the air everywhere we turned. Our schedule was well planned, and upon our arrival we gathered our luggage and began visiting orphanages, schools, and pastors in Port au Prince and surrounding villages.

The poverty there is unimaginable, and it was staggering to see the lifestyle that these precious ones endure. We visited an orphanage that housed countless children of all ages. The only bedding this establishment could afford to provide was cardboard for mattresses. They ate meager rations prepared in pots that were washed with water that ran along the streets, and most of the children had swollen bellies from disease and worm infestation.

Our interpreter was a local pastor who had to walk four miles from his home to join us each day. He then traveled with us from town to town, helping us communicate with those we met. I had packed lots of snacks for Nicholas and me, in case we got hungry between meals. At one point during the day, I realized that I had not seen Pastor Gi eat while he was in our company. "Pastor Gi, have you eaten?" I inquired. "No, I haven't, but I am fine," he answered and smiled. I quickly handed him a package of wafers with peanut butter filling. "Thank you," he said as he took them from my hand and opened the package. We continued to chat in the car as we traveled along, but I noticed out of the corner of my eye that Pastor Gi had eaten only two of the crackers, and was carefully folding the remaining wafers and putting them away. I glanced at the missionary very puzzled, and he whispered, "He's saving the rest of the crackers to give to his family." At that moment, I grabbed my back pack and began to give every snack I had to Pastor Gi. Enough for him and his entire family! He then retrieved his unfinished pack from of his pocket, gave me a huge bright smile and ate. Before we left Haiti, we loaded him and his family with many gifts of food and supplies that we had brought with us.

Many things that I saw that week changed me forever. I saw wonderful men and women who live destitute and in squalor, not complaining, but with joy to further the gospel of Christ. When our trip was finished and Nicholas and I were sitting on the plane bound for Nashville, I thought of our old dinosaur house, and I was thankful. I decided then that I would no longer complain about its electrical problems or leaking pipes, or be ashamed to invite my friends. I decided that our savings were better spent helping the homeless, and those like Pastor Gi and the other Haitian pastors whom we now support.

Do I believe that it's wrong to desire nice things, have lavish homes, or large savings? No, not wrong. I would be lying if I told you that my family would not enjoy a sprawling estate, and maybe one day we will. But I have found brothers and sisters in the body of Christ whose needs outweigh my desire. I have found that my desire to help them outweighs my aspiration to acquire. The book of James reminds us (2:15) "If a brother or sister is naked and destitute of daily food. . . ." Then I ask you . . . *Could I wish some easy life for me?*

A Baby's Cry

This trip with Nicholas was my first trip back to Haiti in many years. I had visited there thirty years ago with friends on a mission trip. I could look in the mirror and see that my looks had changed quite a bit over the time that had lapsed. I've earned every line in my face, and I like to fancy that I'm just more mature with time, and not looking older, but better.

Haiti, in contrast, had changed quite drastically since our last meeting, and time had been less kind. The once lush and tropical nation that I loved was now impoverished and destitute. The pier where our ship had docked so many years ago was now broken down and grown over with weeds. The streets that my friends and I had walked were now littered with burning trash which was being incinerated where it lay. The ocean breeze that we once enjoyed was now filled with the stench of open sewage. I could hardly believe the sight of Haiti that lay before my eyes. As we toured the city of Port au Prince, naked children played along the streets; we witnessed adults urinating on the sidewalks; and saw what once were fine hotels and establishments now abandoned and vandalized. My heart was broken to see the demise of such a beautiful country and the living conditions of its citizens.

We made our way into the compound where we were to stay, and as our car rolled into the driveway, we were met with guards carrying machine guns. I gathered my luggage from the car and walked down the sidewalk to find my room, when my eyes scaled the perimeter of the grounds. I noticed a tall wall made of concrete and boulders that surrounded the property, with all shapes and sizes of glass shards protruding from the top. This wall was certainly not to hold us in, we were guests. It was obviously built for our safety, to keep others out. This I found to be a bit disconcerting; but nevertheless I had committed, so Nicholas and I locked ourselves securely in our room.

To keep us cool, there was a small window unit air conditioner, the kind my grandmother had when I was a child, perched into a hole in the wall. However, there was no air conditioner in the bathroom, so the window remained open throughout our stay. As I stepped to the sink to freshen up from our journey, I could hear the cry of an infant. The "mother" in me went to the open window to see if I could get a look. I couldn't get a glimpse, but how the baby cried!

I was stunned at the poverty that I saw on the other side of the wall. I could not believe the filth and squalor that human beings were calling their home, and I stared out the window for some time, trying to process the information that my brain was receiving from my eyes. And still the baby cried.

I have given birth to two children, had a hand in raising a third, whom I consider my own. We began having children when I was twenty seven, and before I entered into motherhood, I had little tolerance for a crying child. If I heard a baby cry in a restaurant or on an airplane, I instantly looked for another place to sit. In my mind I'd think, "Can't they do something to make that baby stop crying?"

Motherhood changed many things about me. Though I still can't tolerate a baby's cry, I now have to restrain the maternal instinct inside

Kent and Candy Christmas with Haitian orphans

of me that wants to go and comfort the child. I've also noticed that my hearing changed. Now when I hear a cry, my trained ears usually are able to discern whether the infant is sleepy, angry, spoiled, bored, or in pain. I think most parents can do this after a while. We have gone to the aide of crying infants for so long that we become able to determine by the urgency of the tone whether we should run, walk, or take our time in getting there.

As I listened to the cries of this infant, I could hear intense pain. I could hear him screaming for help, but no one seemed to help him. Compassion welled inside my heart, and I thought of his mother who must be sitting close by, wanting so badly to soothe his pain but possibly without the means. Still the baby cried. I tried to comprise a plan to climb the wall, but the glass shards hindered me. I thought, "I'll go around the wall," but I knew my safety was at stake, and I would jeopardize the safety of those around me to take our group deep into the rural community. I was in complete agony as the baby continued to cry.

I began to pray and call upon the Lord to comfort this little one. I began to remind the Lord of his word where he said, "Suffer the little children to come unto me" (Mark 10:14, KJV). I told the Lord that I was bringing this little one before him, and I petitioned him to meet this baby's need.

I have never heard the audible voice of God, but I have heard his still small voice in my heart. He said, "Will you hear the cries of the children of Haiti? Will you have compassion on the poor and orphaned ones whose cries come to my ears? Will you help the children of Haiti?" Immediately, without hesitation, I said, "Yes!" Within days we had obtained property in Port au Prince, and the "Candy House" began. We school, feed, and clothe sixty-five children; twenty-five are orphans and forty are from extremely impoverished families nearby.

When our trip came to a close, with suitcases in hand, Nicholas and I took one last glance around our room. We wanted to remember every detail of our temporary refuge in a foreign land that had forever changed us. Standing still for a moment, I noticed the silence . . . the baby didn't cry.

Homeless Helping Haiti

Helping the poor has long been a way of life in our family. My grandfather was the pastor of a church in a small town in Louisiana, and it seems that he and my grandmother were always taking someone into their home or providing food to a needy family. Both of my grandparents were very benevolent towards the less fortunate, and they were careful to instill this empathy in their offspring.

There was one dear man whom my grandparents cared for whose name was Jack Smith. He lived as a transient, depending much on the mercy of others, as he never possessed the capacity to hold a job or care for himself. Jack was quite a character, and he dearly loved my grandfather and my grandfather loved him in return. Granddad would always see to it that Jack had plenty to eat and a ride back and forth to church. Our entire family embraced Jack, and he is very present in many of my childhood memories.

One outstanding characteristic of Jack Smith was that every time you saw him, he wanted to give you a gift. As a small child I remember that, most every Sunday after church, he would offer me a melted chocolate bar or a smashed pack of gum curved to the shape of his backside. He kept a stash in his back pocket that he had sat on all through church. He was proud to offer them to anyone who would be a willing recipient. He saved his nickels and dimes that were so scarce to buy these treasured offerings. I was just a child, and it never mattered to me that the chocolate was melted or the chewing gum was smashed; I was thrilled to have him as my friend, and even more thrilled to get a treat.

I have often looked back on my memories of Jack with great fondness, and he will never know how he impacted my life. He has now gone to be with the Lord, but I have since learned that he greatly impacted the lives of many others as well. As an adult, I now realize the act of selflessness and sacrifice he made every week to buy gifts for others. He gave all that he had to bring joy to his friends, because he truly loved to give.

Jesus was with his disciples in the Temple watching as the people brought their offerings to God. Many of the wealthy came giving large amounts, but Jesus observes as a poor widow threw in her two mites. A mite was the least valuable coin available at that time. A widow during that time would have had no income, and held the status similar to that of a beggar. Speaking of the rich, Jesus says, "this poor widow has put more into the treasury than all the others. They all gave out of their wealth; but she, out of her poverty, put in everything—all she had to live on" (Mark 12:42-44, NIV). She who gave the least, gave the most in the sight of Jesus.

Upon our arrival back into the states from our trip to Haiti, I could feel the fingerprints of God upon my heart. With all that I had seen, I knew that I was forever changed. I still heard the baby's cries for help outside my window, ringing in my ears. Our flight back into Nashville from Port au Prince had arrived late on a Friday night and on Tuesday night under the bridge I was still carrying Haiti heavily on my heart. I thoughtfully scanned the audience with a renewed awareness of the needs of the poor in Nashville and at the close of the church service,

I began to share with the homeless congregation about my desire to build an orphanage.

I began to tell about the baby who was found in the toilet, whose mother gave birth to him there and left him to die. I talked about the child that was found by a local pastor in a garbage dump, covered with sores and badly diseased. I wanted them to look beyond their own needs and see that there were others who were suffering and even less fortunate than themselves.

As I was speaking, I began to see the homeless as they were moved with compassion. I could see eyes looking back at me that were filled with tears of empathy. I watched as several of the homeless spontaneously got up from their chairs and walked toward me reaching in their pockets. I realized that they were searching for what money they had—change and dollar bills.

I held up my hand as if to say stop. "Wait," I exclaimed. "I'm not receiving an offering, I'm not asking for money. I'm just sharing our plans for an orphanage." But still they continued to come forward. Homeless men and women were handing me their coins and dollars and I tried to stop them to no avail. Finally, most of the congregation had gotten out of their seats and given what they could. I stood there and cried. That night I saw our motley congregation moved with compassion and a desire to help children whom they had never met in a country they may never visit.

That night the offering amount was $42.53, but I believe that in God's eyes it was invaluable. The homeless wanted to give to children who were more needy than themselves, and that is the height of self-lessness. Without being asked, the homeless gave to the helpless. They didn't give out of their abundance, but out of their poverty, and they gave all that they had.

Chapter Ten

Can You See the Clock from Where You Stand?

Prelude

A very popular song when I was a young girl had a thought-provoking lyric: "Does anyone really know what time it is, does anyone really care?" I have often thought of these words, and my answer to this question would be, "I believe that very few people know what time it is."

Many years ago, there was a paper mill in a small town. Every day at noon the whistle would blow to alert the employees that it was time to break for lunch. This whistle was loud enough to be heard all through the factory, and consequently could be heard throughout most of this small town. To insure that his clock was accurate, the foreman would pick up the phone everyday at noon to ask the local telephone operator the time. This went on for several years until one day the foreman asked the operator, "Where do you telephone operators call to find out the time?" The operator replied, "Oh, I set my clock by the lunch whistle that blows every day at our local paper mill. My clock is always right on time." Does anyone know what time it is?

I admit that on a personal level I am a poor judge of time. I am not a particularly neat person; I usually never lay my car keys in one specific place in the house or store my belongings where I know I can find them. It usually takes me quite a bit more time to dress and get out of the house than I estimate, due in part to searching for my car keys. It seems also that I'm not usually accurate when calculating distances with the flow of traffic during a given time of day. Most often I underestimate, and hardly ever overestimate, therefore I am chronically late.

My husband, in contrast, is extremely organized. His things aren't only stored neatly, but colorcoded and alphabetized. He has tried to teach me about time management over the years, to no avail. He jokingly says that he has an easy time staying close to God, because he lives with his thorn in his flesh.

In an effort to be more prompt, I recently bought a clock and hung it on the wall in a prominent location in our house. It is very beautiful, with whimsical figures mounted on its face and Austrian crystals that spin and catch the light. Every hour it plays a tune, and most who visit our home notice it. I have received many compliments on it and felt quite pleased that I had solved my time issues with this new purchase.

There is one small problem with this clock. Its hands are beautifully ornate and gold, which make them almost impossible to see. I've learned that to truly know what time it is, I have to stop what I'm doing, put my glasses on and step in close to the face of the clock, which I rarely do.

Recently, my husband had traveled out of town for several days and was flying back home. I had looked forward to his return, and had planned to pick him up from the airport and take him to our favorite restaurant for a nice lunch. I was excitedly getting dressed, and tidying the house as I went along. I continually glanced at the clock, thinking that I had plenty of time. When I had finished getting ready, I grabbed my purse and ran out the door, jumped into the car, and turned on the ignition. Much to my amazement, when I saw the numbers on the digital clock in my car, I realized that I was not early but actually leaving the house after my husband's estimated time of arrival. I broke all the speed limit laws driving to the airport. When I drove up to the curb, there he stood. As you can imagine, he was less than thrilled and not smiling. This was January, and one of the coldest days of the year for Nashville. Kent was frozen and crestfallen and I could tell that I had hurt his feelings by being late. My actions toward him were interpreted, "She didn't miss me," which wasn't the case at all. In reality, what my actions said was, "I didn't take time to stop, put my glasses on, and stand closer to the clock."

Many clocks say different things, depending on where you are in the world and which time zone you are in. There is also the Doom's Day clock that reads 11:54, six minutes until midnight, suggesting that we are

Kent and Candy Christmas

near the end of time. Yet, two thousand years ago some New Testament writers referred to their time as the "last days" (Hebrews 1:2, Acts 2:16, 17). When I was younger, Christians were always looking for the second coming of Jesus, and much of what we heard coming across the pulpit was about the end of time. I can remember my grandfather's sermons about the end of the world. He believed that Jesus would return "within the next five years," I heard him say. That terrified me. I remember that I was seven years old, and I cried because I didn't want Christ to return when I was twelve; I wanted to grow up to marry and have a family.

In the Old Testament we read, "the sons of Issachar who had understanding of the times, to know what Israel ought to do" (1 Chron. 12:32). I don't believe the sons of Issachar understood the time because they camped out near a sundial, but that they were prayerful and understood the timing of God. The book of Matthew says, ""No one knows about that day or hour, not even the angels in heaven, nor the Son, but only the Father" (24:36, NIV).Jesus understood the "clock" of God, and he begins to give us clues of how to read the signs of the times.

Many of us are so busy racing around meeting deadlines, punching the time clock, and working overtime that we forget to stop to put on our glasses and focus on what time it really is by God's standards. Moments pass that turn into hours, days, and years, and gradually time marches forward to every human being's destination. One day we will all stand before our Maker.

I often think of a plaque that hung on the wall of the church where I attended during my childhood. It was a quote from a poem by a missionary to China, C. T. Studd. It read: "Just one life, 'twill soon be passed, only what's done for Christ will last." We as human beings enter into this world empty handed, and exit taking nothing with us. All we really have is time and the choice of how we spend it. I think that our time on earth should come with a warning: "This is your life, live it responsibly." Does anyone really know what time it is? Do you have your glasses? *Can You See the Clock from Where You Stand?*

Revival in Nashville

After the Civil War, while most of the South struggled to recover from the devastation, Nashville thrived, as farmers, factories, and traders sought out a location close to easier transportation on the river. As Nashville's population began to explode with prosperous people, at the same time, others broke under the pressures of the aftermath of war and the struggle of day-to-day life. Those who struggled sought solace in the hoards of saloons, gambling halls, and prostitution establishments along the Cumberland River. These establishments also became popular forms of recreation for the boatmen who traveled up and down the river.

A group of people who called themselves "Moralists" were greatly offended by all that was wrong, and they began to demand a change in the city. They called upon the great evangelist, Samuel Porter Jones, to come lead a revival. The Methodists built Reverend Jones a tent along the Cumberland River that could hold 7,000 people. As the power of God fell upon the city, Jones held three to four services per day with over-capacity crowds telling folks to "Quit their meanness." During one of the services, a well-known steamboat captain and pillar of Nashville, Captain Thomas Green Ryman, came into the tent with a few of his cohorts wanting to cause a disruption. However, the power of God was so strong under the canvas tent that Captain Ryman and his friends all repented at the invitation of Reverend Jones. Ryman spoke with Jones after his conversion and told him of his desire to build Jones a larger building to hold revivals in Nashville.

In 1892, the doors of the Union Gospel Tabernacle Church (later renamed the Ryman Auditorium) opened to the city of Nashville with a revival. Fifty-one years later, the Ryman Auditorium became the home of the world famous Grand Ole Opry and has played host to some of the most famous musicians and performers in the world.

Now, one hundred and twenty-five years later, we find ourselves along the same river and in the same city still believing in revival.

I truly enjoy reading church history, especially the account of great men of God and their pursuit of revival. I eagerly devour every book I can get my hands on that tells their stories and depicts the settings in which God in his sovereignty visited humanity. I am intrigued with these times of refreshing and seasons of outpouring where the Holy Spirit fell like rain upon those who were thirsty and seeking after him. These have been times when cities and even nations were changed and lives transformed. I have read of Jonathan Edwards and George Whitfield in the 1700s experiencing the Great Awakening; or Evan Roberts and the Welsh Revival of 1904; or William Seymour and the Azusa Street Revival in 1906 Los Angeles.

My heart burns within me as I read these narratives, because I want to see God move again in Nashville and around the world in my lifetime. There are visible signs as well as scriptures in the Word of God that give clues pointing prophetically to an impending revival. I believe that we have entered into a season primed for another outpouring of God's Spirit and a great harvest of souls. "For the earth will be filled with the knowledge of the glory of the LORD, as the waters cover the sea" (Hab. 2:14). "And this gospel of the kingdom will be preached in all the world as a witness to all the nations, and then the end will come" (Matt. 24:14).

In ancient Israel there were seven feasts that were annually celebrated. These were Passover, Unleavened Bread, First Fruits, Pentecost, Trumpets, Atonement, and Tabernacles. The first three occurred in the spring during the time of barley harvest (Lev. 23:10-14).

Barley ripens first and was known as an inferior grain that was eaten by the poor and by animals. Wheat ripened and was harvested later in the spring on the heels of the barley harvest. Wheat was ground into fine flour and eaten by the more affluent, and was twice the price of barley. Usually the poor couldn't afford to buy wheat.

I believe prophetically that there is a great harvest of souls that will be gathered into the kingdom of God before the second coming of Jesus Christ. The laborers in the fields of our Lord Jesus Christ will gather the wheat into the barn, and many will come to the knowledge of the saving power of Jesus. But I see that before the wheat harvest there will be a barley harvest—a harvest of the souls of the poor.

Have you noticed that all of a sudden the world has become socially conscious? It seems that every Hollywood actor/actress, athlete, and celebrity has a cause or charity to champion. More churches than ever before are opening food pantries and have begun outreaches in their communities to feed the poor. Nonprofit organizations are caring for the needs of the poor at an unprecedented rate. God has released a supernatural desire in the earth to help the poor.

Revival is happening under the bridge in Nashville

Why? Because there is a barley harvest coming. I believe there is a harvest of the poor coming to the church. I believe that God will reap the souls that the world has called an "inferior grain," the drug addict, the prostitute, and the alcoholic—the precious ones that many churches reject. They will be changed by the power of God to be made a superior, rich grain of preachers, evangelists, and soul winners We are seeing God moving again, reaching for souls who have fallen into alcoholism, drug addiction, and prostitution. I cannot help but believe that the "time" has come and the stage is set for Music City to have another revival along its streets. I am so convinced of revival that we have built an entire ministry around the verses in Corinthians that say,

173

"But God hath chosen the foolish things of the world to confound the wise; and God hath chosen the weak things of the world to confound the things which are mighty; And base things of the world, and things which are despised, hath God chosen, yea, and things which are not, to bring to nought things that are" (1 Cor. 1:27-28, KJV). I believe that in this time God will again reveal himself to the weakest people of society, those with such simple faith. *Can you see the clock?*

A Timely Message

Each person who comes underneath the Jefferson Street bridge has their own personal story. Some of them had a rough life filled with tragic circumstances, while others had good fortune their entire lives, but never found the fulfillment they continuously sought after. Drug addiction and alcoholism does not discriminate against any race, gender, or social status. But the gospel of Jesus Christ does not discriminate against those who have fallen either. Jude says that "some have compassion, making a difference: and others save with fear, pulling them out of the fire" (1:23, KJV). God impresses upon me the urgency each Tuesday evening to present the gospel to our friends and to lead them to salvation in Christ. I always remind our friends that this particular evening may be their last, as we are not promised tomorrow. Life on the streets is not one that most would ever choose or even dream of living, and that not all of the lives we encounter end happily.

One young woman who was a part of our services, Lil' Bit, was peacefully asleep one evening on the banks of the Cumberland River.

A group of rowdy young men fresh from a night of drinking at the bars downtown decided they wanted to have a little fun. They pushed a sleeping Lil' Bit into the frigid waters of the Cumberland River. When she hit the icy darkness, she became entangled in the blanket wrapped around her and drowned. As the news of her death spread around Nashville, the press came down to the river bank to watch as the authorities pulled Lil' Bit's lifeless body out of the cold river. While watching the news coverage that evening, I watched as they recovered what was left of her personal effects: a Carhart coat, a green gift bag of toiletries, and her sleeping bag, all of which we had given her under the bridge on a Tuesday evening.

We know beyond a shadow of a doubt that our Lil' Bit is in heaven rejoicing at the foot of her Savior, as she had come forward to receive Christ into her heart only a few short weeks before her tragic passing. *Can you see the clock?*

Another young woman who found herself under the bridge was a well-known politician's daughter. She had dined with presidents, governors, and other world leaders. She lived her life in the lap of luxury, but after a car accident, Belle became addicted to prescription painkillers. With marital problems joined to the addiction, she found herself spiraling out of control and checked herself into rehab. During her stint in the rehab program, Belle's husband served her with divorce papers. When he came to pick her up at the end of her stay, he brought all of her worldly possessions in trash bags, drove her down to the riverfront, and left her there to fend for herself. Faced with starting over,

Belle befriended a homeless man who took her to Tent City where she lived for over a year. She heard of The Bridge Ministry and began coming to the services each Tuesday night. When Belle spoke to others about The Bridge Ministry, she would invite them to come and be a part of "her church."

Being a part of the church services gave her hope again for a new start in life. She decided to try rehab once more and checked herself into a half-way house in Nashville. Sadly, the pain of losing everything was too much for her to bear, and she began to turn once more to alcohol to fill the void in her life. Belle died one evening while at the halfway house after becoming so inebriated that she aspirated in her own vomit. *Can you see the clock?*

A joyful young man, Tony began coming to our services in the summer of 2008. You could always count on him for a bright smile or a laugh to brighten your day. He absolutely loved the Carhart clothes that we would give him, and he used them in the construction job he had during the day. Tony had a huge heart and was always quick to lend a helping hand to the volunteers or even to the other homeless who needed assistance. One day in 2009, Tony came forward to receive Christ and signed up to be baptized at the Christmas service a local church was hosting. I remember what an incredibly moving night that was. As the pastor said, "Buried with Christ in baptism; raised to walk in newness of life," you could see Tony's face light up with pure, uninhibited joy. He turned toward the crowd with uplifted arms rejoicing for a fresh start; as I handed him the mic, he sang "Amazing Grace" to the congregation.

A few days later, Tony came up to one of our volunteers visibly shaken. He told the volunteer that he was in debt to a group of men that wanted their money repaid immediately. He did not have the money and now feared for his life. Tony went into hiding, but the men caught up with him and murdered him for not being able to pay his debt. My heart broke at the news of Tony's death, but I knew beyond a shadow of a doubt that he was in heaven. *Can you see the clock?*

Chapter Eleven

I'm Goin' Up

Prelude

Although there is not much information given throughout the Bible about Enoch, we do know that he "walked with God; and he was not, for God took him" (Gen. 5:24).We are told that he was the seventh man from Adam and that he was the father of Methuselah, as well as other sons and daughters. He lived to be 365 years old, and was one of two men, apart from Jesus, who is recorded as being translated or caught up to heaven. The other was Elijah.

There was something special about Enoch, in that he—about whom we know so little—is mentioned repeatedly throughout the books of the Bible. The writer of Genesis makes a point of mentioning that Enoch "walked" with God. I think this is key. The Bible tells us

(Gen. 3:8) that God "walked" with Adam also in the cool of the day, which leads us to believe that this walk was on a more personal level than the walk of faith that you and I walk today. We can assume that, if God walked with Enoch, that this walk was quite possibly much like he walked with Adam.

I believe that God likes to fellowship with people who will believe him, who have the faith to believe his Word. We know that Enoch was a man of faith because his faith is mentioned in Hebrews 11, which is known as the "faith hall of fame." I think God liked to "talk things over" with Enoch. My mind loves to wonder about these things from time to time. It's fun to imagine that maybe the angels are going about their angelic duties, and all of a sudden they realize that they can't find God. I can see one angel asking another, "Have you seen God?" Then another angel pipes up and says, "He's down on earth talking with Enoch again."

We are told that God told Enoch of events on this earth that would come: "And Enoch also, the seventh from Adam, prophesied of these, saying, Behold, the Lord cometh with ten thousands of his saints" (Jude 1:14, KJV). Quite possibly, Enoch is walking with God one day and God begins to unfold his plans for humankind to Enoch. Maybe he comes to the part about the end of this age and tells Enoch, "Son, there'll come a time when the saints won't die, but they'll be caught up in the air." I believe that Enoch's faith grasped hold of this, and he might have said, "I want that, Lord. If you can do that for them, you can do it for me." "By faith Enoch was taken away so that he did not see death" (Heb. 11:5).

The Bible says, "For the Lord Himself will descend from heaven with a shout, with the voice of an archangel, and with the trumpet of God. And the dead in Christ will rise first. Then we who are alive and remain shall be caught up together with them in the clouds to meet the Lord in the air" (1 Thess. 4:16-17a). When I was a young Christian, these passages of Scripture terrified me. I was afraid that I might not be ready, that I might be the one left behind. Now that I have matured in my "walk," I know for sure that when the trumpet sounds, I'll be ready to meet him. There is one fear, though, that I yet carry: "What if those I love aren't ready?" It is my prayer and earnest desire that when I "walk with God and am not," or when I go home to be with the Lord, that my friends from under the bridge are prepared to meet eternity as well.

Many of the homeless are still battling addictions; they are hungry for God, but have not yet made the commitment to surrender to him. I have decided that, if I follow the example of Enoch to take God at his Word, "Ask of me, and I shall give thee the heathen for thine inheritance" (Ps. 2:8, KJV), that God will continue to give us great success in winning souls for him. I stand amazed to see the harvest on the streets of Nashville, where many are coming to the knowledge of Jesus Christ. I love to see hardened hearts melted by the love of Jesus and transformed into that of children of God.

I'm Goin' up . . . . But I don't plan to go alone!

Circus Tales

For most of my life, I have lived from a suitcase, even at home. I was raised traveling on the family bus, singing gospel music, as we toured the country. There was no need to unpack one's bags, just change out the dirty laundry and head back out of town. This was a very exciting lifestyle for a teenager. I was home schooled before home schooling was popular, which gave me the opportunity to be with my family and to see the world.

As I grew older, I married a traveling minister as well as continuing a concert tour schedule. I realized that there are many benefits to being in "mobile ministry," one being that when we arrived back home from a trip, we were able to disconnect the phone line without the fear that our church members may need us in the night. We could live pretty independently.

The downside to being a mobile ministry was, first, that we had not cultivated close relationships in our hometown because we were always away. Second, we rarely saw the fruit of our ministry. If lives were touched or changed as we traveled to other parts of the country to minister, we weren't witness to it. We had already moved on to a different place. In this case, it is easy later in life to feel that your life has been wasted and that your ministry was in vain—which I did feel.

Along with so many other attributes of God that I have seen, I have learned that he is thoughtful and kind. When God gave me this wonderful treasure of ministering to the homeless, he allowed me to see fruit from my labors—to watch as lives are changed through the gospel of Christ.

One cold January afternoon Kent and I decided to go with our children and many friends to the Ringling Brothers circus. A large group of us had decided to go, and because of the logistics of traffic and parking downtown, time ran short and I was not able to eat lunch beforehand. When all of our party had arrived, I announced that I was hungry, so our little crowd migrated to the pizza concession close by. Without closely noticing the server on the other side of the counter, I stood there gazing upward at the menu. I was hoping for some fabulous Chicago-style pizza, which I wasn't finding, so I said, "What is the best pizza you have? I'm starved!" My gaze had turned to the oven by this time, looking for anything besides pepperoni or cheese slices.

"Miss Candy, don't you recognize me?" the server asked, which brought my attention directly to her. There before me stood a pretty young woman wearing a bright red pizza parlor uniform and ball cap. Her face was very familiar, and she was flashing a beautiful white smile from ear to ear. "I am off the streets and drug free. I've had my baby and I got this job at the convention center, and now I have my own apartment." I was amazed. "Thank you for feeding me and praying for me under the bridge. See what Jesus has done for me? Would you like to see a picture of my baby?" Tears welled up in my eyes as I talked with her for a while and looked at pictures of her baby. We had a wonderful reunion.

My husband noticed the lights were dimming in the auditorium and we could hear the ringmaster speaking, and realized the show was beginning. We said our goodbyes and made our way to our seats in the balcony. My daughter Jasmine and her husband JonMichael had gone to a different concession stand, and they met us at our seats. "Mom," she exclaimed, "on our way up here, we stepped into the elevator. The elevator attendant said, 'Hi Jasmine.' I looked up and it was Susan. She works here now. Isn't that wonderful?"

Immediately I recognized the name. Susan was a friend that I went to school with in the fifth grade. I lost contact with her for many years, until one night she resurfaced in my life under the bridge. The first time I saw her, I noticed her from a distance, pulling a ragged suitcase that was filled with all of her possessions. She was homeless and had come to the outreach for food and to enjoy the church service. I didn't recognize her at first, but later that same night as she was leaving she approached me and introduced herself. I was stunned and shaken by the revelation that my childhood friend was living on the streets. I later came to realize that there were mental issues that had lead her to this place in her life. It was very hard for me to accept that our paths from grade school had taken such drastic turns, and that such bizarre circumstances were now bringing us back together. It took me quite some time to recover from the knowledge that my childhood friend was homeless, and I was left feeling very sad, yet humbled and blessed, knowing, "But for the grace of God, there go I."

After helping Susan for several months and watching her increasing devotion to the Lord, she disappeared without a trace from my life again. Until that day at the circus, I had no knowledge of her whereabouts or how she was doing. I had often prayed for her, and hoped that she had found a better life. I was thrilled to know that she was now working and living indoors and doing well.

By the end of the afternoon, we had seen three of our "church under the bridge" members whose lives were better because of Christ. As Kent and I made our way out of the building and back to our car, I could no longer hold back the tears of joy. We talked about all that had happened, and we both decided that the true reason we had gone to the circus that day was not to be entertained, but to see some fruit that our Father wanted us to see. In his kind and thoughtful way, God was saying, "Keep up the good work!"

Often we come into the lives of people at their lowest point, when disaster has driven them from their places of comfort. We love them, encourage them, and offer assistance, but many times when they are back on their feet, they don't return. They don't want to be reminded of the failure and pain they once suffered.

I believe that sometimes the Lord sends "mercy drops" to me, little reminders here and there to say, "Your labors are not in vain." I have made up in my mind to keep pressing on . . . . *I'm Goin' Up!*

The Jeff Stultz Story

Moose is a man that I came come to know very well at the church under the bridge. He is aptly nicknamed, for he is well over six feet tall, a bearded, robust guy with a very colorful personality. He was a faithful church member under the bridge for a couple of years, and is still a shining example of the transformation that can take place in a man's life when he submits himself to Jesus Christ. He was saved under our ministry on the streets, delivered from crack cocaine, and became a staff and choir member of one of the largest full gospel churches in our area.

For a while he played on the fringes of the Christian experience; I noticed that he would attend for a while, then I might not see him again for weeks. I realized that he would be a hard case, and I decided to pray for him, and give him some time, and let God do his work—which he did.

The thing that is outstanding about Moose is his natural ability to influence others around him. He is very friendly with a great sense of humor, and most people enjoy his company. You never see Moose alone; he always has friends around him, and usually he is taking some poor waif under his wing and looking out for him.

One young man whom Moose watched over for a while was Jeff Stulz. When I first came to know Jeff, he was quite a pitiful sight to see. He had contracted a staph infection and was covered with sores from head to toe, and weighed only 108 pounds. You could see by the way he carried himself that the ways of the streets were new to him.

He had been a very successful entrepreneur and business owner, but in 2001 his older sister, who was his best friend, passed away. His grief sent him spiraling downward, which led to his first drug use and subsequent addiction. Within one year, Jeff had lost the woman he loved, his business, and was bankrupt emotionally, financially, and spiritually.

Our good friend, Moose, worshiping

When Moose met Jeff, Jeff was at a very critical time in his life. Moose had found employment with a local congregation and was able to afford a small place to live, so he invited Jeff to stay for a while. Moose frequently brought him to church under the bridge, where seeds of the Word of God were planted in his heart.

Over time I realized that Moose and Jeff had moved on in life, and I saw Jeff less and less. I could only assume that they were doing well, and it was time for the mother-hen in me to let go again. It's a circumstance in my ministry that I have come to accept, that as people progress in life they move beyond the bridge, which is good for them, but sad for me.

A couple of years passed and Kent and I met a local pastor in Brentwood. He had a fatherly way about him and a heart toward the homeless, and inquired often about our ministry under the bridge. As we became better acquainted, I invited him to the bridge and asked him to preach. He readily accepted.

The night came that he was to preach, and I watched as this pastor drove up and parked his car. I noticed that he had not arrived alone, and Kent and I happily greeted him and his guest. "Do you know this man?" he asked. "Well, let me see, he looks familiar," I said, giving my stock answer to that question. "This is Jeff Stulz." I could not believe my eyes! Jeff had gained eighty five pounds, owned his own business, and was preaching the gospel. Jesus turned his life around, and I stood amazed at the awesome power of God in his life. The new Jeff had a bright countenance and a broad smile. I saw a new creature in Christ Jesus, old things passed away, personified.

Today Jeff lives in North Carolina and is on staff at a very large church as "recovery pastor." God has blessed him with a beautiful wife, a successful business, and a home that is completely mortgage free. He supervises Celebrate Recovery for the entire state of North Carolina. The Lord is using him to bring deliverance to the lives of many people.

Let's shout Hallelujah on the streets of gold
I'm going up to see my Lord!

Man of Gadara

And always, night and day, he was in the mountains, and in the tombs, crying, and cutting himself with stones.

Mark 5:5, KJV

My heart is moved when I read about this man of Gadara. He is tormented so much that he has become unable to function in normal society. He is homeless, naked, and living among the tombs in a cemetery. The graveyard that is his home symbolizes what his life has become. His family has been destroyed and his dreams and purpose in life are dead. All that's left that resembles the man he once was are memories that stand like monuments in his mind reminding him of his failures. In his lucid moments he remembers and mourns. At other times he sits cutting himself with stones and bemoaning his wretched condition.

There were those who at times tried to help him or rehabilitate him. Their efforts to tame or restrain him proved unsuccessful. By the time we are introduced to him, his friends and family have given up hope, and he has been left to his own demise. He is left lonely and alone with his cruel taskmaster, Satan.

At this same time, we find Jesus teaching and feeding the multitudes on the other side of Galilee. Suddenly Jesus stops and makes a statement that seems to come from out of the blue: "Let us pass over to the other side." Almost abruptly, he instructs his disciples to disperse the crowd and send them home. It was as if his ears are tuned to a different frequency and he was hearing a cry from across the sea that was inaudible to the others around him. Jesus and his disciples immediately boarded a ship and began their journey to the other side. To the natural eye it seems that he puts greater value on the one whom society has abandoned than his own disciples. In order to reach Gadara, they must pass through a storm and put their lives in peril.

When Jesus and his disciples arrive, the Gadarene ran and fell at Jesus' feet. The invisible power of Jesus did in one moment what chains and fetters could not do. He was subdued without force by the presence of Jesus and fell in worship at his feet. Again and again he begged Jesus not to send his demons, his only companions, out of the area. With only a word from Jesus, the demoniac is freed, the chains of darkness are broken, and Jesus has saved the living from among the dead.

This is an apt picture of many of the homeless that we encounter, people whose potential has been wasted and who have made peace with the demons that have destroyed them. During the times when the Holy Spirit sweeps across our church services under the bridge, I see confusion lift, minds become clear, and men and women begin to worship. When society's efforts have been exhausted through counseling, medication, and incarceration, only the presence of Jesus can set them free. He whom the Son sets free is free indeed (John 8:36).

I think of Thomas, who is such a charismatic young man. He comes from an upstanding family and is very intelligent and well educated. Much of the time that I see him he is raging and out of control on methamphetamines. The police captain over the downtown precinct told me that they often incarcerate him to protect him from himself. Recently Pastor David Miller from Jasper, Alabama was visiting our ministry under the bridge. Thomas cursed him violently, so I gently took him by the hand and led him away as he ranted. The next time I saw Thomas, he was docile and thinking clearly. I am looking forward to the day when he will be loosed from his fetters of darkness and be free.

With feelings of appreciation, the man of Gadara begged to stay in the presence of Jesus. He wanted to board the boat, leaving his past and reputation behind. Jesus said, "Go home to your family and tell them how much the Lord has done for you, and how he has had mercy on you" (Mark 5:18, NIV). I like to imagine what it must have been like the first night he sat down at the dinner table with his family. There he is, clothed and in his right mind, maybe holding hands with his wife across the table. Perhaps his children begin to tell him about their accomplishments at school and bring him up to date with their lives. Whatever the case, there is peace in the house—dad has come home because Jesus has set him free.

One of our precious friends, Ed

This beautiful story of restoration encourages me and gives me hope for the future of the homeless. We have seen many lives changed under the bridge through the knowledge of Jesus Christ. I would love nothing more than for every homeless person in our congregation to be free—and for me to be out of work. But until that day, we are driven by the inaudible cries for help from those that we love so dearly. It is the cry for food from the hungry, for water from the thirsty, and for freedom from the tormented that keeps us working on.

It is in our long-range plan to build a facility where we will be able to house and rehabilitate alcoholics and drug addicts. It is our desire to educate many of the homeless and equip them with job skills where they can become productive citizens again in our community.

I admit that sometimes I may be viewed as a little eccentric or unconventional. Could it be that I'm tuned to a different frequency? Could it be that I hear cries for help from people on the streets ringing in my ears? Could it be that you hear it too? I desperately want these lost and wondering souls to go home and be reunited with their families. I long to see them clothed in their right minds, showing the world what Jesus has done, and the mercy he has shown. *I'm Going Up* . . . . do you want to go too?

A Life-Changing Journey

My husband is quite the outdoorsman. He learned to fish and hunt game at an early age, living on a Native American Indian reservation. I on the other hand, have never cared much for the great outdoors. I'm not a fan of insects or critters that slither, and I find that my hairstyle is more conducive to a climate controlled environment. Kent says that my idea of camping is sitting in the parking lot of The Mall of America in an RV watching cable television and sipping a cappuccino. I quite agree. Imagine the irony of God calling me to a ministry that's out of doors and under a bridge.

Since we were married, Kent has gradually tried to make me a nature lover. Recently, he and I, along with our children, accepted an invitation to spend Thanksgiving weekend with our friends, Mike and Vicky, and their family. They own several hundred acres in south Georgia, and have built a private hunting lodge, complete with cabins and a bunkhouse on the premises. Mike is in the ATV business, so the lodge is equipped with a large fleet of them.

We loaded the car with suitcases, kids, and Chihuahuas, and headed for Georgia. Upon our arrival we settled snuggly into our cabin, then made our way to the dining room to stuff ourselves with a delicious Thanksgiving meal. With my eyes getting heavy, I found myself searching for a comfortable sofa to catch an afternoon snooze, when Mike stood up to make an announcement: "I want everyone dressed and back downstairs by 11 p.m. We are all going for a late night ATV ride." That sounded like a pleasant plan, so about an hour before time to leave, I began dressing. I fired up my curling iron, glued on my eyelashes, and steamed the wrinkles out of my riding ensemble . . . you know, I was getting *dressed*. At 11:00 p.m. sharp we gathered in the front hall, and I noticed that I was met with a few grins from the others, but nevertheless off to the barn we marched. I was shown the four-wheeler that was to be mine for the night, so I placed my protective eyewear over my eyes, and started the motor.

Mike led the way, in what looked to me like a golf cart on steroids; it was some new ATV he was test-driving, and the rest of us filed in line behind him. There was a caravan of fourteen ATVs in all that night, and the roar of their engines was deafening, which only added to my excitement. My heart raced as we began maneuvering up a steep mountain; having never driven an ATV before, I admit I was afraid. When we reached the mountain's peak, we sped down into a valley, and I went squealing all the way. We drove through thickets and brush so dense that at times we stopped for Mike to hack tree limbs with his machete to gain passage. We roared through creeks with mud slinging all over us. I never gave another thought to my appearance—I only had survival on my mind! I realized that I wasn't driving the ATV, it was driving me, and I held onto the handle bars of that thing for dear life. Aside from God and family, I can truthfully say that I have never had a better time in my life.

We did not know that Mike was leading us to a destination he had previously visited; we simply thought we were on a random excursion through the woods. As we rode deeper into the woods, a light came into view in the distance. As we approached, we could see that it was a bonfire built on the banks of a river. Mike had sent someone ahead of us to prepare a little oasis in the wilderness. Upon our arrival, we cut our engines one by one until all that could be heard was the crackling of the fire in the quiet night. Vicky served up cups of hot chocolate as we made makeshift seats around the fire out of logs and pieces of driftwood. The full moon lit up the cloudless sky that teamed with brilliantly shining stars, providing a magical setting for making memories between our two families. There in the night we formed bonds of love and friendship that can never be broken, as we shared stories and sang songs and laughed the hours away. That Thanksgiving journey was life changing for me.

After our trek back to the cabin, I kicked my muddy boots off at the door and made my way to the mirror to survey the damage. Much to my horror, my hair was slicked straight back forming one large dreadlock that was caked with mud! From head to toe I was covered in dirt. All I could see glaring back at me were my two white raccoon eyes that were visible after removing my protective eyewear. I was a scary sight to behold, and I didn't even care.

You might say that, in a sense, this story is also the story of my journey under the bridge. At the onset, I really had no way to anticipate or prepare for the adventurous ride on which I was embarking. Although it has been the trip of a lifetime, it has certainly taken me trudging up mountains and whirling down through dark valleys. Because of my inexperience, I admit that I've often been afraid. There have been impasses along the way, and I've often had to stop to hack through them in prayer. But God always made a way. I've gotten my hands and face dirty, and at times I might have had a little mud slung on me. Even with all the ups and downs, I can tell you truthfully that, aside from God and family, I've never had a better time in my life.

Yeah, I look in the mirror and I admit that I'm not quite the same as when I started, and I don't even care. Somewhere along the ride I got my eyes off of myself, and I got my eyes on the survival of others. I just keep holding on tight to the handlebars, knowing that I'm not really doing the driving, that I am being driven and I'm just along for the ride. I'm can hardly wait to see all the places God is taking me. Whatever the destination, I know he has gone before me, because every Tuesday

I arrive at an oasis in the wilderness. It's not a place that's prepared only for me, but it's for the hundreds of volunteers and homeless—all the *family* of God who gather there.

As spiritual darkness covers our land, on the banks of the Cumberland River the fire of the Holy Spirit burns brightly. We are warmed as we share and laugh and sing praises together under the bridge, and bonds of love are formed between us that can never be broken. Above all other roads I've traveled, this journey is life changing for me.

Afterword

Now that you and I have traveled the road to the bridge together, I hope that you have seen just how easy it is to reach out to others at any level. Maybe you are sitting there just like I was, thinking, "I want to reach out. I want to do something to help my fellow man. I want to make a difference in my community, and most of all I want to work for the Lord. I just don't know where to start."

Jesus said, "Go ye into all the world, and preach the gospel" (Mark 16:15, KJV). Many times I read this passage of Scripture thinking that I must travel to foreign fields to fulfill this great commission. I now feel much more enlightened by seeing that the "world" is actually in the grocery store checkout line next to me or playing with my children in my backyard. We can share the message of Jesus Christ and his love in any corner of the world where God has placed us.

Can I tell you that I have never felt so fulfilled or more happy in my life than I do now? You might say that under that seven-lane bridge in the heart of Nashville, Tennessee, is my "happy place" on this earth. A place where I have seen the face of Jesus in my homeless friends, and I will certainly never be the same. "Inasmuch as you did it to one of the least of these My brethren, you did it to Me" (Matt. 25:40).

I read a medical study written by Dr. Stephen Post, a professor at Case Western Reserve University, where he states that helping others and doing good deeds releases an endorphin in your body that makes you feel happy, even euphoric. He likened it to a drug high. Remember, I was depressed. So, reaching out to others has changed my life and has given me joy that can hardly be contained or completely expressed within the pages of this book. You see, the fact of the matter is, the homeless have done far more for me than I could ever do for them.

So, are you convinced? Are you ready? Would you like to help? No, not help me. Help you. Help others. Help Jesus. You are more than welcome to come to Nashville and help me in the warehouse, or help me on the streets. In the future, we are planning a learning center to help educate the homeless to get better jobs and earn better wages. This learning center will also include a free clinic for the homeless to receive healthcare, and eventually have housing for many more than we have now.

I am thinking there is a bridge in your city, or a soup kitchen, but more importantly there are wonderful people waiting to hear the good news. My grandmother used to say, "There's no time like the present." If you will reach out your hand and begin your journey of faith, I believe that God will surprise you in many ways. You will see that there is a blessing . . . *On the Other Side.*

Get involved!

www.bridgeministry.org

The Bridge Ministry, Inc. • PO Box 463 • Goodlettsville, TN 37207 • (615) 228-3437

Music by
Candy Christmas

on the other side

There is a Blessing (On the Other Side)
Since I Laid My Burdens Down • Can You
See the Clock • Troubles of This World
Jesus on the Mainline • Orphans of God
Jesus Built This Church on Love • Climbing
Up the Mountain • Could I Wish • Precious
Lord (Take My Hand) • I'm Going Up
Jesus on the Mainline (Bonus Cut)

HYMNS OF HEAVEN
first love

Draw Me Nearer • My Jesus, I Love Thee
I Shall Know Him • 'Tis So Sweet • Eastern
Gate • How Beautiful Heaven Must Be In
the Sweet By and By • Sweet Beulah Land
It Is Well • Turn Your Eyes Upon Jesus
Precious Memories • Wonderful Peace

Available at your local bookstore or online at:
www.candychristmas.com